JEFF GORDON

NASCAR'S DRIVEN SUPERSTAR

Jenna Fryer and
The Associated Press

Mango Media
Miami
in collaboration with
The Associated Press

  AP EDITIONS

AP Editions

Published by Mango Media, Inc.
www.mangomedia.us

This is a work of non-fiction adapted from articles and content by journalists of The Associated Press and published with permission.

Jeff Gordon *NASCAR's Driven Superstar*
ISBN: 978-1-63353-353-0

Publisher's Note

AP Editions brings together stories and photographs by the professional journalists of The Associated Press.

These stories are presented in their original form and are intended to provide a snapshot of history as the moments occurred.

We hope you enjoy these selections from the front lines of newsgathering.

"Honestly, I've had so many distractions over the years, far more distractions than I've had this year, and performed well."

— Jeff Gordon at Darlington Raceway on September 4, 2015, commenting on speculation that the weekly celebration of his career at each NASCAR stop may have led to distractions.

Table of Contents

PREFACE

The request came via text message in the middle of the 2014 offseason. Jon Edwards, who has done the public relations for Jeff Gordon for as long as I've known them, was inquiring about my travel plans for a January sports car race. I let him know what day I was leaving — and then forgot about the exchange. A few weeks went by and Edwards asked me if I was available to go to a dinner with Jon Bickford, Jeff's stepfather, the night before I was due to travel. I said I didn't like to go out and leave my daughter before I go away for the weekend, and that night did not work for me.

The next communication came by phone call from Jon. He said "John Bickford really wants to do a dinner that night; there's a chance we can make Jeff available at the dinner. Does that change things?" I asked why it had to be that night, and Jon said "it's the only time Jeff is available." Now this bugged me. Jeff has always been a consummate professional and maintained a pretty regimented schedule. His personal time was his personal time, and in the 15 years I'd known him, he didn't permit his personal time to be interrupted. After the birth of his two children, he became even more protective of his days off. So it bothered me that I was being asked to give up my personal time with my daughter at a time that was inconvenient for me just for the convenience of Jeff Gordon.

I asked Jon if I was missing something, why this urgency to sit down with Bickford and Gordon? Jon told me it was to "discuss a new business venture that they were going to be involved" in together. I eventually decided discussing a business venture wasn't worth the sacrifice and told Jon I could not attend the dinner.

Two weeks went by and I was driving to the airport to leave for that sports car race. It was the morning after the night they had wanted to go to dinner. An email popped up on my phone from a Hendrick Motorsports account I did not recognize. I immediately opened it.

Jeff Gordon was retiring at the end of the season.

I wanted to drive my car into a ditch and hide from the utter humiliation of realizing that Gordon had tried to give me the story a day early. I was devastated. I got on my plane, landed in Daytona Beach, Florida, and while I was still in the airport parking lot, Jeff called.

He opened with, "Man, Jenna, I thought I was going to be telling you this news over a nice bottle of wine."

We talked nearly 30 minutes, and during that time, he received a text from his mother that brought him to tears. He choked out the words as he read it to me. "I never knew watching SportsCenter could be so emotional," she had sent him.

Gordon has always been emotional, unafraid to hold back tears. He cried after his first victory in 1994, cried during his first championship acceptance speech a little more than a year later and cried after many crowning moments in a storied career that included 93 victories, four titles and a marketing appeal that changed NASCAR forever.

He sobbed as he told his Hendrick Motorsports team his retirement plans that January morning, and the moments continued to collect until the end of the 2015 season. In his final task as a NASCAR driver, Gordon was celebrated during the December awards ceremony in Las Vegas.

NASCAR called on Tom Cruise to do the honors, and Gordon began to openly weep the moment the actor was introduced.

"He felt as comfortable discussing a championship with George Bush as breaking down Homestead with Kyle Busch, as at-ease with discussing SNL skits with Jimmy Fallon as racing door-to-door with Jimmie Johnson," Cruise said. "And with that, he brought joy to millions, used his immense and deserved popularity for the betterment of the world both at home and abroad.

Transcendence. Few reach it. He did. And although many of us want to say we'll miss you, what we really mean is we thank you."

Cruise nailed it because Gordon had indeed broken every barrier and ended many of NASCAR's stereotypes after he arrived on scene.

Born in California, he was in a quarter-midget by age 5. Bickford raised him to be professional, to be a good sport and to be fair on and off the race track. As he tore through every local series, Gordon needed to find a series that challenged him. Bickford picked sprint cars, but local racing officials refused to allow a 14-year-old to compete in what many consider to be one of the most challenging cars in auto racing.

So Bickford moved the family to Indiana, where the age criteria was not as stringent, and Gordon's career was now on a launching pad to superstardom.

It took Gordon just four years to prove he was a bona fide star, and his effort was helped by ESPN's "Thursday Night Thunder" series that showcased USAC races. Gordon had an unbelievable 1990 season, winning four of the "Thunder" races while reeling off six of his first seven races in the USAC Silver Crown Series.

He claimed the National Midget title that season, and was in NASCAR the next year. He drove in what was then called the Busch Series for Bill Davis. He won three races at NASCAR's junior varsity level driving for Davis, but their relationship was short. Gordon was snatched up by Rick Hendrick in late 1992 and he made his Cup Series debut on the last day of that season as the torch was officially passed. Gordon's debut race came in the final race for seven-time NASCAR champion Richard Petty.

It was just a footnote at the time, but as Gordon established himself as the most dominant driver of the 1990s, the irony of him running his first race on the same day as Petty's last is no longer debated. Gordon finished 31st that day, crashing after 164 laps.

He began to find his footing in 1993, his first full Cup season. Gordon finished fifth in his first Daytona 500, grabbed 11 top-10 finishes and earned rookie of the year honors. He was a winner the next year in a very big way: Gordon's first career Cup win came in the storied Coca-Cola 600, the longest race of the year, and at Hendrick's considered home track of Charlotte Motor Speedway.

His next win was monumental. In NASCAR's first trek to Indianapolis Motor Speedway, Gordon won the debut 1994 race for his second career win.

As he reminisced over the 2015 season about his highs and lows, he considered that win at The Brickyard the highlight of his career. He ultimately went on to win at hallowed Indianapolis a record five times. He also won three Daytona 500s and championships in 1995, 1997, 1998 and 2001.

This explosion of talent was packaged so differently from the typical NASCAR image. Bickford had raised Gordon to dress professionally, to have stellar manners, to be a gentleman and to be able to handle himself on the race track and in a boardroom.

He was a new breed of driver, so clean-cut and polished that he immediately raised NASCAR's corporate image beyond its moonshine roots. NASCAR was suddenly a legitimate power on Madison Avenue as tens of thousands of new fans flocked to automobile racing in the late 1990s and 2000s.

Gordon became such a household name that he even hosted "Saturday Night Live" and was name-dropped in a song by rapper Nelly. He did it all while dominating as the "Rainbow Warrior" and teaming with crew chief Ray Evernham to collect checkered flags at a record pace.

The ride, though, wasn't always smooth.

Gordon fell in love with model Brooke Sealey, then Miss Winston Cup, in 1994. She was forbidden to date drivers, so their romance was a secret. They soon married and Gordon made a hard shift in his career. He cut ties with Bickford, the stepfather who had managed his career since he was 5, and ventured into new avenues with his business.

It created a schism between Gordon and his parents, and as Gordon's fame grew and grew, he and Brooke began to live a very isolated life. Behind all the smiling victory lane celebrations was Gordon's growing dissatisfaction.

He felt badly for the way he handled things with Bickford, regretted cutting people from his life, and felt little joy after leaving his 2001 championship celebration.

Gordon's wife was barely visible at the opening race in 2002, and it didn't take long for the entire industry to realize his marriage was on the rocks. An announcement that the two had split came early in the season, and it garnered unprecedented attention in the tabloids. But Gordon used the time for a reset on what he wanted out of life.

He reconnected with old friends, repaired his relationship with his family and brought Bickford back on to run Gordon's business entities. He dated several women, then found his true love in Belgian model Ingrid Vandebosch. They have two children together, and Gordon is a doting dad.

Gordon treasures his family, and some of his most memorable career moments are from celebrating with daughter Ella and son Leo. His dramatic final victory in November 2015 came with a tremendous amount of pride.

Gordon won at Martinsville Speedway in Virginia to claim one of the four berths in NASCAR's championship-deciding race. He celebrated as if it was his first career victory, and embraced his children as they savored the magical moment.

Alas, there was no storybook ending. Gordon was a mediocre fifth in the finale and couldn't contend with ultimate champion Kyle Busch.

As his career came to an official end, there was no regret. Instead, he reminisced about a career that has given him a fulfilling and remarkable life.

"There's no such thing as a perfect day and a perfect life," Gordon said. "Just like there's no such thing as a perfect race car. I think had I won this race and this championship it would have been perfect, and I don't think I could have accepted that. I wouldn't have known how to," he said after his final race.

He also touched upon a private moment he shared earlier that morning with his mother.

Gordon intended to spend his final morning as a race car driver somewhat solitary and certainly low key. When he opened the blinds on his motorhome that morning, his mother just happened to be passing.

He invited her in.

"She walked in, and we started hugging and talking, and I just started thanking her over and over and over again for all that they did for me," he said. "And then we got off to a completely different subject, just talking about my sister and family and life and what's going on here and there and just stuff like that, had a coffee. We had coffee together.

That just made my day start so amazing, to be able to sit down with her on that day, first thing in the morning, and all the emotions and everything were just able to come out, and then we just had a great conversation. And then my step-dad came in and then a little bit later Ingrid and the kids showed up. It was just perfect."

Now it's on to new projects for Gordon, who opened the 2016 season as an analyst for Fox Sports. The job makes him part of NASCAR's weekly circus, still gives him relevance in retirement.

Away from the track, he's busy as well with humanitarian work that has been universally lauded as exceptional. The Jeff Gordon Children's Foundation was launched in 1999 and has raised close to

$20 million. The foundation now focuses singularly on fighting pediatric cancer. In 2006, he helped open the Jeff Gordon Children's Hospital in Concord, North Carolina.

In 2011, he visited the Congo on behalf of his own foundation and the Clinton Global Initiative, dedicated to charity work ranging from eradicating cancer to ending hunger. And in 2012 Gordon traveled to Rwanda to celebrate the opening of the Butaro Cancer Center, the first specialized cancer treatment center in the country. Gordon was joined in dedicating the facility by Former President Bill Clinton and Rwanda President Paul Kagame.

The Jeff Gordon Children's Foundation donated $1.5 million to the center that now boasts an emergency department, a full surgery ward with two operating rooms, and significantly expanded laboratory capabilities, among other necessities.

"That's what we're dealing with in Africa," Gordon said. "Saving lives."

After two trips to Africa in one year, Gordon reflected on why he felt so strongly to be a humanitarian.

"We work so hard out here to try and win and put so much effort into it," Gordon said. "Yet, 10, 15 years from now, what is it all going to mean? Those trophies are nice, but they do tarnish. When you try and save a life ... those are the things that stick with you for a lifetime."

With a new television career and his charitable acts, Gordon has more than a fair share on his plate. But he's still a highly-regarded celebrity and the consummate spokesman. He's appeared on every morning show, most of the late night shows, and has co-hosted with Kelly Rippa. He remains the only NASCAR driver to appear on "Saturday Night Live," which he hosted.

So what else is there for Gordon? He's a lock for the NASCAR Hall of Fame on his first ballot. His victory total trails only Petty and David Pearson, both Hall of Famers, on NASCAR's all-time wins list.

There was a period in his career when it looked certain he'd end his career atop every category. But his shot at adding to his championship total was altered when NASCAR changed its point system in 2004. Not long after, Hendrick teammate Jimmie Johnson, who had been practically hand-picked by Gordon to become his team-mate, began a run of dominance that saw him reel off five consecutive titles and six in seven years.

Hendrick will forever credit Gordon for being an integral part of building the preeminent team in NASCAR. The two developed a bond over 23 years together and credit each other for their successes. When a Hendrick plane crashed into a Virginia mountain en route to a 2004 race, an accident that killed 10, including Hendrick's son, brother and twin nieces, it was Gordon who steadied his boss when Hendrick lacked the enthusiasm to face his employees.

Gordon remained loyal to the Hendrick brand and his boss for his entire NASCAR career, and the two could settle most issues with a handshake.

In the moments after he climbed from his car following his final race, Gordon shared a quiet moment with Hendrick next to the car. He presented Hendrick with a helmet that had been designed specifically for that race.

"You know, I don't know whether he's like a younger brother or a son, but it's both the same. He's family to me. I love him like he was my brother or my son. He has been there for me, and I've been there for him," Hendrick said. "When you can deal with a professional athlete and you can go 23 years and you don't need a lawyer, you can take a handshake, and we've never had a disagreement, I think that's tremendous respect for each other.

"He's a rare commodity. I'm just thankful that we're going to still be together and still do things together, hopefully do more together, and he'll have time and maybe I can slow down, he can help me take a load off of me, but he's just special, and I couldn't care for anybody any more than I do for Jeff Gordon."

— Jenna Fryer

Jenna Fryer began working for The AP in college at West Virginia University. She was hired full-time in Montgomery, Alabama, where she spent three years covering the SEC, Alabama and Auburn. She transferred to Charlotte, N.C., in 2000 to cover the NFL's Carolina Panthers and the NBA's Charlotte Hornets. Her first exposure to NASCAR was in Alabama, where she attended a race at Talladega. Fryer's coverage of NASCAR widened in Charlotte, the hub for most NASCAR teams, and she was thrust into a central role of The AP's coverage following Dale Earnhardt's death in the 2001 Daytona 500. In 2006, her primary focus became auto racing and she currently spends the bulk of her time covering NASCAR and IndyCar out of Charlotte. Jenna is also a major contributor to AP's "Under the Hood" and the writer of "In The Pits," a weekly auto racing column.

INTRODUCTION

Jeff Gordon watches after the final practice for Sunday's NASCAR Sprint Cup series auto race at New Hampshire Motor Speedway in Loudon, New Hampshire., September 26, 2015. (AP Photo/Jim Cole)

THE IRON MAN OF NASCAR
Loundon, New Hampshire, Sunday, September 27, 2015

Jeff Gordon kissed his wife and high-fived his two young children on pit road, a part of his life missing when he made his Cup debut in 1992.

What has been familiar for all 23 years of Gordon's career was starting a NASCAR race in the No. 24 Chevrolet for Hendrick Motorsports.

He's never missed one - and now he's NASCAR's new Iron Man.

Gordon's latest milestone in a surefire Hall of Fame career came Sunday at New Hampshire Motor Speedway when he set the NASCAR record with his 789th consecutive start. The 44-year-old Gordon passed Ricky Rudd for the record. Rudd set the mark in 2002 when he broke Terry Labonte's streak of 655 consecutive races.

"Jeff's a good guy, so if someone's going to break the record, better him than not one of your favorites," Rudd said by phone to

The Associated Press. "I've done my time. People still remember me. I may not be Iron Man 1. Maybe I'm Iron Man 2 now."

Gordon will retire at the end of the season and shift in 2016 into the Fox broadcast booth.

The four-time Cup champion's streak began with his Cup debut on November 15, 1992, at Atlanta Motor Speedway. He has never missed a race and holds the record for the longest consecutive starts streak from the beginning of a career.

Should Gordon make every start the rest of the season, he'll have 797 consecutive starts.

Gordon has four series championships and his 92 wins have him third on the career list, trailing only Hall of Famers Richard Petty (200) and David Pearson (105).

Gordon and his family took a parade lap around the New Hampshire track in a duck boat usually reserved for Boston's champions.

"It's rare that we get the team and my whole family and they get to ride around the track with me like that, so that was very special," Gordon said.

Gordon's first race came in the last one for Petty, now a team owner. The Atlanta race was won by another Hall of Famer in Bill Elliott, whose son Chase will replace Gordon next season at Hendrick Motorsports.

Gordon was saluted Sunday by baseball's Iron Man, Hall of Famer Cal Ripken Jr. Ripken started 2,632 straight games for the Baltimore Orioles - like Gordon, he set the streak with one team.

"Congratulations to Jeff on an amazing career," Ripken said. "His love of his sport shows in the way he races and the fact he is about to become the 'Iron Man' of racing. His ability to compete at the highest level of such a demanding sport for so long is a testament to his passion and skill."

Rudd, who had 23 wins and never won a championship, methodically built his streak from 1981 to 2005 and won at least one race a season from 1983 to 1998.

Rudd, who once taped his swollen eyes open so he could drive, said he never thought any driver from his era would last long enough to break his record.

"I knew it was possible, but with the kids that come in today because they're so young," Rudd said.

Gordon's durability has been as remarkable as anything else. He's had a balky back for the latter part of his career and it nearly ended the streak last season at the Coca-Cola 600. He cut short his practice runs because of back spasms and there was some concern if he could race. Team owner Rick Hendrick even had backup driver Regan Smith on standby.

Gordon started and gutted out all 400 laps.

Rudd said Gordon has benefited from racing in an era where the cars and tracks are safer.

"You have to pat NASCAR on the back for catching up on getting these cars safer," Rudd said. "For me, that's the one thing that will make the record more beatable in the future. It seems like it would be a rarer situation where a guy would get a concussion compared to years ago."

New Hampshire was a fitting venue for Gordon to become the new Iron Man. He is the only driver to compete in all 41 Cup races there and leads all drivers in top-five finishes, top-10s, laps led and laps complete at the 1.058-mile track. He finished seventh on Sunday and is 10th in the Chase for the Sprint Cup championship standings.

Chapter 1

FINAL CHAMPIONSHIP

Jeff Gordon drives the final lap of the UAW-DiamlerChrysler 400 at the Las Vegas Motor Speedway. Gordon won the race for his 53rd victory, March 4, 2001. (AP Photo/Eric Jamison)

COMING ON LATE FOR VICTORY
Las Vegas, Sunday, March 4, 2001

This was the Jeff Gordon that everyone remembers, working with his team to perfect his car and blowing away the field in the end.

Gordon, NASCAR's biggest star now that Dale Earnhardt is gone, came up with the right combination late in Sunday's UAW-DaimlerChrysler 400, took the lead with 20 laps remaining and drove off to an easy victory at Las Vegas Motor Speedway.

"It was a little frustrating at the beginning," Gordon said. "The car was real, real tight in traffic and we were just struggling."

Gordon's team, led by crew chief Robbie Loomis, kept working on the balky handling in his No. 24 Chevrolet and a two-tire stop late in the 267-lap race on the 1 1/2-mile oval was the key.

"That freed the car up quite a lot and all of a sudden it came to life," Gordon said, beaming at Loomis - the man who had the difficult job of replacing longtime Gordon crew chief and mentor Ray

Evernham. "I was going by guys that had four (new) tires and just walking away from them after that."

All the leaders pitted on lap 179 during the last of six caution periods of the race, and, with the two-tire stop, Gordon, who went into the pits sixth, came out third behind Hendrick Motorsports teammate Jerry Nadeau and the Dodge of Sterling Marlin.

Marlin took the lead on lap 202, and Gordon got by Nadeau for second on the next lap. Gordon stalked Marlin, cutting steadily into his lead before charging past on lap 225 to become the 12th different leader in the race.

Gordon lost the lead for a while during a series of green-flag pit stops, but came back out on top on lap 248 and pulled away from the second-place Ford of Dale Jarrett to win by 1.477-seconds - about 15 car-lengths.

"That showed me and this entire team that we have to stick together and never give up," Gordon said. "It's some-thing we need to keep doing every race."

It was Gordon's first victory since last September in Richmond, Virginia. Besides the regular first-place money, he got a $1 million bonus from series sponsor Winston.

"Winning at this racetrack today, as much as we've struggled here in the past, it means almost as much to me as the million dollars," said Gordon, who had finished 28th, third and 17th in the previous Winston Cup events here.

Last year was particularly frustrating, with Gordon crashing in practice on Saturday and never being competitive in the race with the repaired Monte Carlo.

"We fixed the car instead of going to a backup and then, when we got home, we found out the frame was bent," Loomis said. "It was terrible, terrible, terrible. When you're sitting on top of that (pit) box and Jeff Gordon is going from 10th to 40th, that ain't good."

The three-time series champion said the victory proves to him that his team is capable of racing for another title this year.

"If we can run this strong at a track like this, we're off to a good start," he said. "We just need to keep doing what we're doing and build on the momentum."

The win also broke a string of three straight Las Vegas victories by the Roush Racing Fords of Mark Martin and Jeff Burton.

Jarrett said the Fords continue to race with an aerodynamic disadvantage this season because of rule changes that have given the other makes an edge.

"You can really feel it when you pull up on another car like Gordon's Monte Carlo and your momentum just stops," the 1999 series champion said.

Jarrett, who started from the pole, added that his car became very loose late in the race.

"We got a set of tires where the car just went crazy loose and that kind of spooked me," he said. "We never got it back free enough and it never let me race Jeff."

Johnny Benson finished fourth in a Pontiac, followed by the Fords of Todd Bodine and Martin and the Chevy of last week's winner, Steve Park - the best finish among the three Dale Earnhardt Inc. entries. Daytona winner Michael Waltrip was strong early but faded to 13th, while Dale Earnhardt Jr. led briefly and slipped back to finish 23rd.

Kevin Harvick, who replaced the elder Earnhardt at Richard Childress Racing after NASCAR's biggest star was killed in a crash on the last lap of the Daytona 500, was the top-finishing rookie. He was eighth.

Burton, who won the race here the last two years, was the first driver eliminated from contention when he lost control and hit the wall on lap two.

"I wasn't on the gas or anything, and it started coming around and I never could pull it back," said the bewildered 39th-place finisher. "I do not have a clue what happened."

Another early crash knocked Penske Racing teammates Rusty Wallace and Jeremy Mayfield out of the event. Others involved in wrecks on Sunday were Joe Nemechek, John Andretti, Hut Stricklin and Mike Wallace.

The victory was the 53rd in the career of the 29-year-old Gordon, tying Rusty Wallace for the most among active drivers.

WINNING THE WINSTON IN BACKUP CAR
Concord, North Carolina, Sunday, May 20, 2001

Jeff Gordon's second best car turned out to be good enough to win The Winston.

Gordon, in a backup car because his primary one was damaged during a wreck at the start of the race, came from the rear of the field early Sunday to win NASCAR's all-star race.

It was Gordon's third victory in the race, tying him with the late Dale Earnhardt for the most wins in the event.

"I don't think you can tie him in anything - he's just above and beyond anything that I can accomplish in a race car," Gordon said of the seven-time Winston Cup champion. "He did very special things in our sport and it's awesome to be a part of it."

The race was delayed 2 hours, 10 minutes because of rain, but not before NASCAR tried to start the event on time despite light drizzle.

The track was wet and slippery by the time the green flag dropped, and as the cars came out of Turn 1, many of them lost control and began to slide.

Kevin Harvick lost control of his car and hit the wall heading into Turn 2. The cars behind him tried to slow, but Gordon couldn't avoid running into the back of Jeff Burton's car.

The tap sent both cars spinning, and as Gordon shot down the track, Michael Waltrip slammed into the side of his car.

NASCAR quickly put the yellow flag out and pulled the cars off the track as the rain continued. Officials ruled that because a full lap had not been completed, the race did not officially begin.

That meant Gordon, and the three others, could turn to backup cars. Gordon did, although it meant he had to drop to the back of the field when the race re-started.

No matter.

He had moved up to fourth by the end of the first 30-lap segment and followed Tony Stewart across the finish line at end of the second segment.

"When the second segment started, they dropped the green and I just knew the car was strong," Gordon said. "I can't say enough about the adjustments the crew made from the minute we went to that backup car. They just got it right."

Jeff Gordon holds up the trophy in victory lane after winning The Winston NASCAR race at Lowe's Motor Speedway in Concord, North Carolina, May 19, 2001. (AP Photo/Chuck Burton)

Gordon pitted and took four tires before the final 10-lap shootout. He was second on the re-start, but needed less than a lap to pass leader Ward Burton, who had taken only two new tires.

He then easily held off Dale Jarrett, beating him to the finish line by 0.701 seconds to win the race and earn the $515,000 first prize. It was the 10th victory for Chevrolet in the 17 runnings of the event.

Jarrett, who has yet to win the race in 10 tries, was the runner-up for the second consecutive year. He earned $125,000.

"It's nice to finish second, but this race is not about second, it's about winning," Jarrett said. "I thought we had a shot at it but I couldn't get a run on Jeff on the re-start. It was a good run for us, but we'd really love to win this thing."

Stewart, who won the second 30-lap segment to earn a $50,000 bonus, was third in a Pontiac and won a total of $160,000.

Stewart's teammate, Bobby Labonte, was fourth, followed by Jerry Nadeau and Burton.

Dale Earnhardt Jr., last year's winner, was seventh. Todd Bodine, who made the 21-car field by winning one of two qualifying races before the main event, was eighth.

Johnny Benson, the other qualifying race winner, was ninth, and Bobby Hamilton rounded out the top 10.

During the rain delay, Gordon said he doubted he would be able to win the race in the backup Chevrolet his team had just taken off the hauler. But that didn't stop him from dreaming.

"I said, 'Wouldn't it be something if we can win this thing in a backup?'" Gordon said. "I didn't think it would actually happen, but we did it through awesome teamwork."

Jeremy Mayfield won the first 30-lap segment to earn a $50,000 bonus.

The field was then inverted, with the last 12 cars in the field being brought to the front for the start of the second 30-lap segment

That meant Elliott Sadler, who finished 12th in the first segment, was moved to the front of the pack for the start of the second.

But Sadler couldn't hold the lead, giving it up to Benson four laps into the segment. Benson fared no better, losing his position to Stewart with 12 laps to go.

Stewart held off Gordon the rest of the way to win the second segment.

The three other cars involved in the early wreck didn't fare nearly as well as Gordon.

Harvick was knocked out of the race early in the first segment because his brakes locked up. His car fell off the pace and he pulled it onto pit road, where it came to a stop and had to be towed away. He finished 21st.

"I mean, when it's not you're night, it's not your night" Harvick said. "At least we didn't wreck this car, though."

Jeff Burton finished 16th.

Waltrip ended up 20th, and was none too pleased with NASCAR.

"In NASCAR's haste to put on the show, it seems as if we perhaps started the race on a wet track," Waltrip said. "My prized Chevrolet is torn all to pieces and I'm not too pleased about that."

WINNING AT DOVER
Dover, Delaware, Sunday, June 3, 2001

Jeff Gordon knows nothing is certain in racing, so he wasn't enjoying the beating he was giving the rest of the field Sunday at Dover Downs International Speedway.

He was too busy counting the laps, hoping he wouldn't have to turn on to pit road for a splash of gas that would enable him merely to finish the MBNA Platinum 400 as something other than the winner.

"I was thinking it would be a real shame to lead that many laps and lose it at the end," he said after holding off Steve Park for the victory. "I just didn't want to get caught up in a fuel-mileage deal."

That has happened twice to Gordon at Dover, most recently in 1999, when he led 375 of 400 laps then was forced to go in for gas and watch helplessly as Bobby Labonte drove to victory.

"It doesn't matter how great you are all day long," Gordon said. "The only lap that counts is the last one."

This time he was in front at the checkered flag after leading 381 laps while re-establishing himself as a force at Dover. He also ended Tony Stewart's bid for three straight wins on the track.

"This is the best car I've ever had here," Gordon said. "We could stay out in front even after the tires went away."

It was the second victory this season and the 54th overall for the three-time Winston Cup champion, tying him with Rusty Wallace and Lee Petty for seventh-best in NASCAR history. It also was the fourth win for Gordon on one of NASCAR's most difficult tracks.

But Gordon said it wasn't as easy as it seemed.

"I know it might have looked like the car was on a rail, but there's no easy way around Dover," he said. "If you listened to the scanner it might have sounded like I was complaining."

The victory ties him with Bill Elliott and Ricky Rudd for the most by an active driver at The Monster Mile, where Bobby Allison and Richard Petty won seven times each. Stewart, trying to join Gordon, David Pearson and Wallace with three straight Dover victories, finished seventh.

"We just didn't do everything we needed to today," said Stewart's crew chief, Greg Zipadelli.

His counterpart, Robbie Loomis, was all smiles when asked what about calling the shots for Gordon.

"He's a crew chief within himself," said Loomis, in his second season with Gordon. "Hendrick Motorsports gives us great cars, but Jeff Gordon's the icing on the cake."

Loomis laughed when asked if he's ever been involved in a 381-lap spanking.

"Sure," he said. "But I was always on the other end of them."

Gordon won here for the first time since sweeping the races in 1996. He began his run of three straight Dover victories in September 1995. Stewart won both races last year.

Dale Jarrett, who won the pole on the basis of points when qualifying was rained out Friday and is nursing a cracked rib from a crash in practice May 26 at Lowe's Motor Speedway, wound up fifth. He leads the series standings by 50 points over Gordon.

"I'm worn out, but Jeff wore us all out," Jarrett said. "Our car was probably a little better than the driver today."

The race was run under mostly sunny skies after two days of bad weather prevented qualifying and cut into practice time.

Gordon's Chevrolet beat that of Steve Park by 0.828 seconds, giving the 29-year-old driver from Indiana his 11th top-10 finish in 17 career starts on the high-banked concrete oval.

"Park gave me a good run there at the end, but we had the right setup," Gordon said.

Park was looking for his third career victory, but after closing within a half-second late in the race was unable to catch Gordon.

"Jeff was just driving the wheels off the thing, and so was I trying to catch him," Park said.

Dale Earnhardt Jr. made it a top-three sweep for Chevy in the $3.6 million race. Ricky Craven was fourth in a Ford, giving 2-year-old PPI Motorsports its best result ever.

Craven, a former Gordon teammate who led three times during exchanges of pit stops, started thinking about celebrating his first career victory as he listened to crew chief Mike Beam on the radio.

"Mike is saying, 'You're six back ... you're five back ... you're four back,'" Craven recalled. "For a brief moment I thought, 'What am I going to say in Victory Lane?' I shouldn't have done that."

Gordon, who started second, led five times, and averaged 120.361 mph. The race was slowed for 31 laps by five caution flags.

There were 16 lead changes among eight drivers.

Rudd finished 10th, Wallace 21st and Elliott 40th.

GORDON BACK NEAR TOP
Brooklyn, Michigan, Wednesday, June 6, 2001

When Jeff Gordon won for the first time this year, he climbed out of the car, turned to his crew and emphatically shouted, "We're back!"

That was just over two months ago, and with two more victories in the last three weeks, Gordon again is a dominating force.

"To be competing for a championship right now - it means more to me to be a part of this team than it ever has," he said. "I can honestly say this is the best it has ever felt."

The driver once known as The Kid isn't so young anymore. He'll be 30 in August, enabling him to better appreciate his quest for a fourth Winston Cup championship. It took almost two years of struggle for Gordon to work his way back to being a threat to win each week.

He won the last of his championships in 1998, then fell to sixth in the standings when crew chief Ray Evernham left to start his own team. After the 1999 season, most of his heralded pit crew, the Rainbow Warriors, jumped to Dale Jarrett's team.

New crew chief Robbie Loomis came aboard in 2000, and Gordon slumped to ninth in the series standings - his lowest finish since 1994 - and won just three times.

"I was really burned out," he said. "This schedule is so hectic. Throw on top of it all the responsibilities of being a champion and there's no doubt it takes a lot out of you."

But the struggle eventually made him hungrier, and now everything is back on track. He's proven that in the last three races.

He won The Winston, NASCAR's non-points all-star race, in a backup car last month. A pit-road accident relegated him to a 29th-place finish in a very fast car the next week in the Coca-Cola 600.

Then he rebounded to lead 381 of 400 laps Sunday in Dover, Delaware He chose not to contest a bonus-points pass by Rusty Wallace early in the race, immediately passed him again, and was out of first thereafter only when he pitted.

It was Gordon's 54th career victory, tying him for seventh place with Wallace and stock car pioneer Lee Petty.

Now, with renewed energy, Gordon heads into this weekend's K-mart 400 in second place, just 50 points behind Jarrett. Last year, Gordon was 10th, 340 points behind Bobby Labonte.

"It was awful tough to go through those tough times and face the criticism and the doubts that everyone has," he said. "So to finally have it clicking and get it together and finally get a team back out there winning races and battling for the championship, it's very gratifying."

Loomis and the rest of the crew first sensed it from Gordon back in March, when he scored his first win of the year in Las Vegas.

"I'll never forget it, he got out of the car and screamed," Loomis said. "It was the most affirmative show of support he'd ever given this team and it made us think we really are going to be on this year."

Loomis, who started as a crew chief in 1991 with seven-time champion Richard Petty as the driver, also has sensed a new confidence in Gordon as well as a new appreciation for the three titles he won with Evernham.

"Now that Jeff is 29, I think he's at the point where he's really starting to appreciate the things he has and the things he wants," Loomis said. "I think when he looks in the mirror, he's starting to see a really good driver.

"During his championships, I think maybe he looked in the mirror and saw Hendrick Motorsports, Ray Evernham, a good car, good motors and a good crew. Now what he sees back is how important he really is to the process."

Others also see how important Gordon and his resurgence are to NASCAR's success.

Petty, the NASCAR pacesetter with 200 victories, says the death in February of Dale Earnhardt, has left a void in the sport.

"Gordon was like Earnhardt, it's a love-hate deal," Petty said. "The people that didn't like Earnhardt or his ways of doing things, they could go with Gordon because Gordon is the smooth part of everything that was the rough part about Earnhardt."

Petty also thinks someone is needed to carry the sport the way he did before seven-time champion Earnhardt became its superstar.

"When I came along there really wasn't a bad guy in the crowd and it worked," Petty said. "I took it from one level and put it in another level. Earnhardt picked it up from there."

Petty has no problem figuring out who should carry on now.

"To me, Gordon, is the head honcho," The King said.

GORDON WINS KMART 400
Brooklyn, Michigan, Sunday, June 10, 2001

If there were any doubts that Jeff Gordon is back to championship form, he answered them Sunday with a milestone victory.

Gordon survived a bad final pit stop that forced him to slice his way through the field, a pair of restarts and a tense battle with Ricky Rudd over the final two laps to win the Kmart 400 at Michigan International Speedway and give Hendrick Motorsports its 100th victory.

"That's a true mark of a championship-caliber team - to be able to stay calm, regroup and come back in," Gordon said. "That's what we did and that's why this team is so good."

Gordon, coming off two straight disappointing seasons, won for the second consecutive week and the 55th time in his career, and took the points by 26 over Dale Jarrett.

And it put Rick Hendrick into the record book as just the third car owner with 100 victories. Petty Enterprises has 271 and Junior Johnson 139.

Jeff Gordon holds up the winner's trophy in victory circle after winning the NASCAR Kmart 400 at Michigan International Speedway, June 10, 2001. (AP Photo/Craig Williby)

But Hendrick couldn't be at the track to celebrate the win. His father, "Papa" Joe Hendrick, is scheduled to have heart surgery on Monday. So Hendrick remained in North Carolina to be with him.

So the three Hendrick cars, including Terry Labonte and Jerry Nadeau, donned stickers on their Chevrolet's that said, "Get Well Pop."

"The only thing that takes away from this win right now is that we couldn't have Rick and Pop here," Gordon said. "But I know Rick was excited. He was thrilled and he would have loved to have been here."

Gordon was off to another dominating performance - he led 137 of the first 174 laps - when an error on the final pit stop cost him the lead.

He led Rudd and Sterling Marlin into the pits on lap 175 but came out sandwiched between them. That's when his crew radioed him to come back in because the lug nuts were loose.

Rudd, who had his own tire problems, followed him in and, after a second stop, the two went back on the track in 10th and 11th place with Marlin as the leader.

But they zigzagged their way through the field - running three-wide across Michigan International Speedway at times - and were right behind Marlin when a caution came out on lap 189.

"I made some pretty incredible moves to get by some cars," Gordon said. "I only know one way and that's to go for it. When you've got a good car, you've got to put in on the edge."

It returned to green-flag racing with seven laps left, and Gordon got a tremendous jump on the restart. He passed Marlin in Turn 1, taking Rudd with him.

"We had a good car on the long runs, but he could beat us on the get-go," Marlin said. "We ran in the corner on the restart and the car wouldn't stick. Jeff got by us and I knew that was it."

Moments later, Shawna Robinson, the first woman in a Winston Cup race in 12 years, brought out the seventh caution flag of the race with a spin in Turn 2.

After two laps under caution, NASCAR returned the field to green with four laps left.

That's when Gordon and Rudd began their stirring duel.

Rudd looked to make a pass several times, then made his move coming out of Turn 4 with one lap to go. His Ford Taurus went high on the track and looked past Gordon, then changed direction by sliding low and passing Gordon's Chevrolet on the inside inches before the finish line.

Gordon wasted no time in retaking the lead, sweeping up high on the track in Turn 1 to pass Rudd. He then drifted down the track to block Rudd from making another move and held him off around the track and at the finish line by .085 seconds.

"It was just everybody for themselves at the end and we came up second," Rudd said. "The mistake I made was I went in front before the white flag lap. If I had made my move later, I maybe could have held him off. But once he got past me, I knew it was over."

Marlin finished third in a Dodge and was followed by Jeremy Mayfield, Ryan Newman and Hut Stricklin.

Robinson, in a Ford Taurus splashed with pink paint, finished 34th.

"It's better to finish 34th than have a torn-up car," Robinson said. "I'm here to learn and I did that."

SLOW START BUT THIRD BRICKYARD WIN
Indianapolis, Sunday, August 5, 2001

As Jeff Gordon lined up to start the Brickyard 400, the last thing he expected was a victory.

The Winston Cup series leader knew he didn't have the fastest car on the track to begin the race Sunday and never thought it would be good enough to make him the first three-time winner of one of NASCAR's biggest events.

"We started the race with a lot of doubts in my mind, that's for sure. I thought I had the slowest car out there at one time," Gordon said, laughing.

He can afford to joke around now. After some great pit work by his Hendrick Motorsports crew, Gordon, who turned 30 a day earlier, surged to the front and celebrated his birthday with a checkered flag, solidifying his lead in the championship chase.

"Well, I had to win it because my crew chief was going to wring my neck if I didn't because I was chewing him out so bad at the beginning of the race," the three-time Winston Cup champion said.

Crew chief Robbie Loomis and the rest of the crew spent most of the 160-lap race on the Indianapolis Motor Speedway's 2 1/2-mile oval making adjustments on the No. 24 Chevrolet.

"I said to Robbie, 'I want to be careful to not get this too far out of whack on our setup because I think all we need to do is just get up front.' And I believed if we got the track position we'd be pretty good," Gordon said.

Jeff Gordon kisses the champions trophy after winning his third Brickyard 400 at the Indianapolis Motor Speedway, August 5, 2001. (AP Photo/Michael Conroy)

They got it right just in time.

A two-tire pit stop gave Gordon track position and he took full advantage, passing gambling Sterling Marlin for the lead on a restart 35 laps from the end.

With a full house of 320,000 spectators jammed into the vast speedway grandstands - many of them cheering for the former Indiana resident - Gordon was able to control one more restart and stay out front for the 56th victory of his Winston Cup career.

"At the end, when we took two tires, it was absolutely the perfect thing to do," Gordon said. "The car drove great once I got out front. This is the best way of celebrating my birthday."

Gordon, who started 27th in the 43-car field, didn't break into the top 20 until nearly a third of the race was gone.

"You start the race with a car as bad as we did today and get a win like this, man, that's special," said Loomis, who became Gordon's crew chief at the start of the 2000 season.

Marlin, running a fuel strategy that would have allowed him to run to the end without stopping, took the lead when all the other lead-lap drivers pitted during a caution period on lap 132.

"It was our only shot to win the race," said Marlin's crew chief, Tony Glover. "You can't line up eight or ninth and win the race."

Gordon and several others took only two fresh tires and Gordon came out of the pits just behind Marlin in second. On the restart on lap 136, he drove his Chevrolet to the lower edge of the race track and raced past Marlin's Dodge.

"We had been leading earlier in the day and running in the top five and I thought we could hold him off," Marlin said. "But it took the car a couple of laps to get going on restarts."

He got one more shot at Gordon after Jerry Nadeau's crash on lap 139 brought out the last of seven caution flags. On the restart on lap 143, though, Marlin got bottled up behind the lapped car of Todd Bodine.

"Unfortunately, a car was trying to get a lap back and he got between Gordon and me and that was tough," Marlin said. "If we could have got by Todd I think we could have worked on him a little. I missed a gear on that one and got too far behind. We give it all we had the last 20 laps and just came up short."

Marlin, hoping to give Dodge its first victory since its return to NASCAR's top series after a 16-year absence, wound up matching John Andretti for the best finish so far by the new Intrepids.

Gordon, who previously won the inaugural Brickyard in 1994 and again in 1998, was able to cruise the rest of the way, beating Marlin to the finish line by 0.0943 seconds - about 10 car-lengths.

The winner earned $428,452 from the race record purse of $6.75 million. He averaged 130.790 mph in the race slowed by 28 laps of caution.

Johnny Benson and Rusty Wallace, who also took only two tires on the last stop, finished third and fourth, followed by rookie Kurt Busch and Ward Burton.

Steve Park, who was leading before the last stop and appeared to have the strongest car most of the day, wound up seventh.

It was Gordon's fourth win of the season, matching Dale Jarrett for the series lead.

With Jarrett failing to lead a lap and falling back to 12th in the late going, and Ricky Rudd getting hit with a mechanical problem that left him 39th, Gordon extended his series lead to 160 points over Jarrett and 179 over Rudd. Rudd came into the race second, trailing by just 45 points.

Park led three times for a race-high 39 laps, while Gordon led twice for 29.

"I a little disappointed," Park said. "The last pit stop just got us a little bit behind and, with only 20 laps to go and a bunch of cautions, there wasn't enough time to work out way back up front.

"My hat's off to Jeff Gordon. Those guys made the right call."

SETTING NASCAR RECORD
Watkins Glen, New York, Sunday, August 12, 2001

The first time Jeff Gordon saw Watkins Glen International, setting a record here never entered his mind.

"I thought this was one place I'd never win at," he said.

Now, after making history, it seems like he can't lose.

Gordon became NASCAR's King of the Road, setting a record Sunday for road-course victories by winning the thrill-packed and attrition-filled Global Crossing.

"You start working on shifting and braking, and pretty soon you're in victory lane," he said after his fourth trip there in the last five years at Watkins Glen.

Jeff Gordon celebrates after winning his fourth NASCAR Winston Cup Global Crossing in five years at Watkins Glen International, August 12, 2001. (AP Photo/David Duprey)

The three-time Winston Cup champion won for the seventh time on a road course, breaking a tie with Rusty Wallace, Richard Petty and Bobby Allison for the most in history.

Gordon's victory also extended his lead in the points race to 194 over fourth-place finisher Ricky Rudd.

But it wasn't easy - right to the end. Jeff Burton, with whom Gordon waged a magnificent battle over the final laps, hit him coming to the final turn.

"If he wanted to, he could have taken me out," Gordon said. "I like racing him with because he's hard, aggressive and clean."

Burton thought Gordon had the better car and credited Gordon's talent for helping him win the race.

"I gave him a good shot coming off the last corner but he didn't even budge," Burton said.

Patience had much to do with Gordon's victory, and he had said he would not try to press for the lead at the outset.

And, some early problems convinced him that was good strategy.

"The brakes were running a little hot and the pedal was going down to the floor," he said. "We had to pump them for the rest of the day."

Gordon had the lead for only one lap before passing Burton in the first of 11 turns on the 78th of 90 laps. Burton got the lead back on the next turn, but Gordon beat him through the chicane, making a great save as the cars nearly touched and almost spun.

"He drove in there too deep, and I was surprised he didn't spin out," Burton said.

"I didn't know if I was going to make it, either," Gordon said.

There were two more cautions, but each time Gordon got a good jump on the restart.

Gordon said Burton was going very slow hoping to get a run at him each time the green flag came out.

"He was hanging back so far I finally took off," Gordon said. "I thought NASCAR was going to say I was jumping the restarts."

Still, he had a close call that enabled Burton to close in on the final lap.

Elliott Sadler had hit the wall, and his badly bent car was still running - in the path of the leaders - as they neared the final turns.

"Elliott Sadler was all over the place, and I was just trying to be cautious," Gordon said. "But Jeff wasn't because he wanted to win the race."

It was a record-setting fourth victory for Gordon on the 2.45-mile course. He also has won three times on NASCAR's only other serpentine layout, in Sonoma, California.

Gordon benefited more from staying out of trouble than fast racing. Wallace had mechanical problems and was out after 14 laps, polesitter Dale Jarrett spun out on the 18th of 90 laps, road-racing ace Ron Fellows stalled on lap 36 and a fire in a telemetry box caused hard-charging Robby Gordon to quit on lap 59.

That left only Jeff Gordon, Rudd and Burton as serious contenders.

But Rudd lost his chance when Boris Said, one of several road-racing aces in the field, made a mad dash toward the front after the race went green on the 84th lap. He passed three cars, then banged Rudd out of the way to take third place.

"Boris just went in there and drove right over the top of us," Rudd said. "We're lucky he didn't wipe out the whole field.

"Everybody was slipping and sliding, and it looked like a Saturday night short-track race."

It was the second straight victory for Gordon, who also put his car in the winner's circle seven days earlier in the Brickyard 400 at Indianapolis. The 30-year-old Gordon has 57 victories, the most among active drivers.

Gordon's Chevrolet started 13th in a field of 43 and officially beat the Ford of Burton by two car-lengths. The victory was his fifth this year, breaking his tie with Jarrett.

The winner led 14 laps. He averaged 89.801 mph in a race slowed six times by 14 laps under caution.

Jeremy Mayfield was third. Rudd was followed by Todd Bodine. Gordon was the only non-Ford driver in the top five.

There were 13 lead changes among 11 drivers.

Jarrett also went off the course later in the race when he was hit by Mark Martin, and fell to third in the standings, 265 points behind Gordon after a finish of 31st.

Wallace, a three-time winner here, wound up last. Fellows finished 42nd and Robby Gordon 40th.

HE'S BACK
Kansas City, Kansas, Sunday, September 30, 2001

After two years of rebuilding his team and his confidence, the dominating Jeff Gordon is back.

The three-time Winston Cup champion solidified his points lead Sunday with his series-leading sixth victory of the season, pulling away from rookie Ryan Newman to win the crash-filled Protection One 400 at Kansas Speedway.

Gordon had to survive a wild 267-lap event on the 1.5-mile tri-oval that saw 13 caution flags and an 11-minute red flag stoppage before earning the 58th win of his career and his third in a first-time event.

Newman, who passed series runner-up Ricky Rudd for second place five laps from the end, wound up trailing Gordon's No. 24 Chevrolet to the finish line by about five car-lengths.

"The secret is a team led by Robbie Loomis," said Gordon, praising the crew chief who replaced his former mentor Ray Evernham after the 1999 season. "They put an incredible car under us.

"This team is really good at new tracks, getting a lot of information and adapting quickly to a new environment. That's what has gotten us here battling for another championship and winning races."

Gordon, who won his titles in 1995, 1997 and 1998, has also won inaugural races in Indianapolis in 1994 and Fontana, California, in 1997.

Rudd held off Rusty Wallace and Sterling Marlin in a three-wide battle for third at the finish. After gaining 130 points on Gordon in the last two races, Rudd slipped 10 back and now trails by 222 with eight races remaining.

The fourth-place finish was a big disappointment to Wallace, who led a race-high 118 laps but had to come back from 17th in the late going after being penalized for speeding off of pit road.

With cool temperatures - highs in the low 70s - and a new track, the race was punctuated by crashes. The only reported injury was to Dale Jarrett, who collided with Bobby Labonte and slammed into the concrete wall on lap 247.

The 1999 series champion was transported by helicopter to nearby Kansas University Medical Center for examination and observation after briefly losing consciousness in the crash. He was awake and alert and walked to the ambulance with help from safety workers after being removed from the car.

Jeff Gordon celebrates following his win in the NASCAR Protection One 400 at Kansas Speedway, September 30, 2001. (AP Photo/Dick Whipple).

Jarrett sustained a concussion and bruised the left side of his chest. He was released from the hospital Sunday night.

After blown engines took out contenders Bill Elliott and Johnny Benson, it appeared Wallace and Gordon were going to battle to the finish as they ran 1-2 late in the race.

Wallace ran into trouble, though, after Dale Earnhardt Jr., winner of last Sunday's race in Dover, Delaware, blew a tire and smashed into the turn two wall on lap 229, bringing out the ninth caution flag.

All of the lead lap cars made their final pit stop for gas and Wallace was caught speeding as he tried to get past Mark Martin at the end of pit road after making his stop.

Meanwhile, Rudd, who had been hanging around the rear of the top 10 most of the second half of the race, chose to take no tires and beat everyone back onto the track. Gordon, who took two tires, fell to fifth.

Another blown tire sent Matt Kenseth into the wall on lap 239 and that kept the field tight behind Rudd, with Gordon moving up to third, just behind Martin. On the next restart, on lap 245, both Martin and Gordon shot past Rudd and Gordon then took the lead for good the next time around.

Rudd followed the leader and retook second and began to close on Gordon before Jarrett's crash brought out the yellow again. By this time, Wallace was up to eighth.

On the restart on lap 256, Wallace shot to the outside of the track and passed three more cars, but his momentum was slowed when rookie Jason Leffler, who started from the pole, collided with Terry Labonte, hit the wall on the main straightaway and prompted NASCAR to red flag the event to be sure it would finish under green.

The cars, stopped on the backstretch, were refired after 11 minutes and 6 seconds and the green flag waved for the final time with six laps remaining.

Wallace made another outside move and got past Martin to fourth, but was unable to get any closer.

Meanwhile, Newman, his new Penske Racing teammate, went after Gordon, but the Ford driver was not able to put any real pressure on the veteran.

"We had a good car, a top-two or top-three car, all day long," Gordon said. "I hate that for Rusty. It was a tough break for him, but I also think we had something for him there at the end."

Newman crashed in practice on Friday and wound up driving a spare car, which was the one in which he won the pole for an ARCA race here in June. He credited the car with the strong finish.

"My car refired better on colder tires than the other cars, but I never expected to get past Ricky like that be able to hang with Jeff at the end," said Newman, who is running a handful of races this season and will run for Rookie of the Year in 2002.

Asked about all the crashes, Newman said, "It was partially this being a new racetrack. It's not just the surface, it's drivers adapting to it. If you go someplace like Charlotte, unless you're a rookie you already know what to expect. But the track really came around to us halfway through the race and we were able to get two-wide and even three-wide racing."

ERNHARDT AND PETTY IN HIS SIGHTS
Hampton, Georgia, Monday, November 19, 2001

As Jeff Gordon hoisted the mammoth trophy, the spoils of another Winston Cup championship, he ditched a much heavier burden.

Yes, he could win a championship without his mentor.

Yes, he could bounce back from one of his worst seasons.

Yes, he deserves a place alongside Dale Earnhardt and Richard Petty.

Gordon clinched his fourth Winston Cup title Sunday at Atlanta Motor Speedway, cruising to a sixth-place finish in the NAPA 500 while Bobby Labonte was winning the race.

For Gordon, this was all about redemption.

He won his first three championships with Ray Evernham as crew chief. After Evernham left to run his own team at Dodge, Gordon slumped to ninth in the standings last year.

Naturally, there were plenty of people who wondered if "Wonder Boy" could regain his dominance.

"What I like about the criticism is that it motivates me and this team to go out and prove them wrong," Gordon said, savoring another championship on a cool fall night. "There were some tough times. To see these guys stick together and come back as strong as we did this year makes me really proud."

Here's something else that should make him proud: Gordon got his fourth season championship a lot quicker than Earnhardt and Petty, the only other drivers to win that many.

Petty was 35 when he captured his fourth title, Earnhardt 39. Both went on to claim three more championships apiece in their storied careers.

Gordon turned 30 in August. He's only been racing in Winston Cup for nine years. While one can't get caught looking too far ahead in life-and-death world of racing, the march to seven championships - and beyond - appears inevitable.

"When you see Jeff Gordon at 30 years old, how mature he is in the car, and you see the chemistry of this team, I think we're going to win a lot of championships," car owner Rick Hendrick said. "I'd like to say we're going to win seven or eight championships. That's certainly our goal."

The Gordon-Evernham team dominated Winston Cup from 1995-98, winning three championships and finishing second the other year. Their reign peaked in 1998 with a 13-victory season, tying Petty's modern record.

Evernham left during the 1999 season, and Gordon slumped to sixth. Last year, Robbie Loomis took over as crew chief and the Rainbow Warriors broke in a bunch of new people in the garage. The result: only three victories and a drop of three more places in the season standings.

Gordon had not finished that low since his rookie season of 1993. He was downright uncomfortable when they got to the season-ending banquet.

"Me and Robbie were sitting at that No. 9 table in New York," Gordon recalled. "The speaker was blowing us out. We couldn't hear each other talk. We made a promise to each other that we would not be sitting at that table the next year."

Hendrick is impressed with the way Gordon held the team together through the tough times.

"He kept his head up last year when everybody was writing us off," Hendrick said. "You hear other drivers all the time saying their car is no good. But he shouldered all the responsibility."

With Earnhardt's death at the season-opening Daytona 500, Gordon is clearly the biggest star in the sport. Yet, all that success at such an early age appears to have spawned a degree of jealousy among his competitors.

Just listen to Sterling Marlin, who is 14 years older and hasn't come close to winning his first championship.

"Jeff is a great driver, but he stepped right into one of the top rides when he came in," said Marlin, who finished second in Sunday's race. "He had Ray Evernham with him. When you surround yourself with good people (and) ... you get good equipment, you can go."

In a symbolic touch, Gordon wrapped up the title on the same day that Labonte, last year's champion, took the checkered flag. Jerry Nadeau held a commanding lead until he ran out of gas on the final lap, allowing Labonte to streak by coming out of turn four.

Marlin and Kevin Harvick also passed Nadeau, who limped across in fourth place.

By that time, Labonte's tenure as champion was over. Gordon ensured himself of enough points with five laps to go, the moment marked with a banner above his pit stall.

Labonte was more gracious than Marlin, but still the conversation turned to Gordon beginning his career at age 21 with a first-rate team.

"He started off with good equipment. There's nothing wrong with that," Labonte said. "He realizes he's where he's at because of that. He could have been on one side of the fence saying it was all him."

Still, it's funny how no one said Earnhardt won all those championships because he had a strong team. The conversation usually centered on The Intimidator's fearless, aggressive, never-give-an-inch style of racing.

Gordon has all of those same attributes, but perhaps it gets lost because he comes across as such a goody two-shoes away from the car.

"When the car is right, he drives the wheels off it," Labonte said. "He can take a good race car and make it a lot better than the other guys can."

Gordon doesn't care how he's perceived in the garage.

"I'm not one to go out and say I'm the greatest or I want to be the greatest," he said. "I just want to be part of the greatest team. I'll say that till I'm blue in the face."

TEAM LEADER AND CHAMP
Wednesday, November 21, 2001

Jeff Gordon was the student and Ray Evernham the teacher. The product of their collaboration was 47 victories and three championships.

When Evernham became restless and decided it was time to take on projects of his own, Gordon was left to fend for himself.

After so much success in their seven years together, it was thought that Gordon might flounder without Evernham.

The large anti-Gordon faction among NASCAR's fans expected - and hoped - the brilliant Rainbow Warrior would become a faded talent without his mentor.

Forget it, Gordon haters. This guy is just too good.

And now he's in Loudon, N.H., for the season finale as a four-time champion. Only the sport's biggest icons - seven-time title winners Richard Petty and late Dale Earnhardt - were more decorated.

Moreover, Gordon has matured into a leader on his No. 24 team. He has stepped into the role left vacant when Evernham departed late in the 1999 season to start his own team and direct Dodge's return to the Winston Cup series this season after a 16-year absence.

Gordon has become the same kind of mentor to crew chief Robbie Loomis, who moved into Evernham's job at the start of the 2000 season.

"When Ray left, there was somewhat of a void," Gordon said. "He was a very outspoken leader, and Robbie wasn't there yet. Everybody was kind of waiting for someone to step up and I felt like it was up to me. Now I do feel like more of a part of the team.

"I know more about the inner workings and I know I'm not going anywhere."

Not next season - never. Last year, Gordon signed a lifetime contract with team owner Rick Hendrick.

The owner, who also campaigns Chevrolets for Terry Labonte and Jerry Nadeau, was surprised things worked out so quickly for Gordon's team.

Jeff Gordon, left, shares a laugh with crew chief Robbie Loomis after winning the NASCAR Save Mart 350 race at Sears Point Raceway near Sonoma, California, June 25, 2000. (AP Photo/Ben Margot)

"You look back at this team at the end of '99. The pit crew left, the crew chief left, the best fabricator left," Hendrick said. "I thought it would take longer to build the team back, but some things just fell into place, and Jeff Gordon showed his maturity level and stepped up again."

Gordon won his first three championships in 1995, 1997 and 1998, and finished second to Labonte in 1996. Then, with Evernham planning his departure, the team slipped to seventh in the points in 1999.

Last year was even worse, with Gordon sinking to ninth in the standings.

The worst moment came in Las Vegas in Loomis' third race with his new team.

"We ran absolutely terrible," he said. "When you sit on that pit box and you have Jeff Gordon driving for you and you fall back to 35th, you just want to disappear."

The driver wound up 28th that day, and the struggles continued for a while. Eventually, though, the rebuilt team began to hit on all cylinders late in 2000.

"I guess that wasn't a very bad year for most teams, and I felt like we were making progress," said Loomis, recruited away from Petty Enterprises by Gordon. "We worked together and grew through our failures and struggles."

Gordon echoed Loomis, saying he considered the season a bad one because he knew what this team was capable of accomplishing. But Gordon wasn't surprised by the comeback in 2001.

"The people who thought we were going to stay down are overlooking the whole picture," he said. "Hendrick Motorsports has so many resources. Even though we had a lot of changes, there's a lot of depth on this team."

The team spent 2000 trying new combinations and looking forward.

"Points didn't mean anything to us," Gordon said. "We wanted to improve the car, improve our pit stops, improve our communications. The last 10 races of last year, things really came together.

The momentum continued into 2001, with Gordon leading the series with six poles, six wins, 24 top-10 finishes and by far the most laps led.

Now Gordon is a four-time champion with 58 career victories. And, at the age of 30, he might not have reached his prime.

"Jeff Gordon and Robbie Loomis make a great team," Hendrick said. "They have that magic in a different way. They like working together and I don't think they will burn out.

"Considering Jeff's age and the chemistry the team has now, I'd like to say we can win seven or eight championships. That's our goal."

Gordon doesn't want to think that far ahead. He's just enjoying the present.

"I love being a champion," he said. "I've learned how to enjoy the responsibilities and expectations that come along with that. You can either fight them or seize them.

"Winning races is great, but there's nothing like winning championships."

Chapter 2

PASSING THE TORCH

Jimmie Johnson, left, is congratulated by car owner and fellow driver Jeff Gordon, right, after Johnson's qualifying laps at Lowe's Motor Speedway in Concord, N.C., May 23, 2002. (AP Photo/Nell Redmond)

CROSSING TO BUSINESS SIDE OF RACING
Concord, North Carolina, Tuesday, September 18, 2001

NASCAR champion Jeff Gordon crossed over to the business side of racing on Tuesday as part owner of the Chevrolets Jimmie Johnson will drive next season.

Gordon joined Rick Hendrick, owner of his Winston Cup team, as the leadership for Johnson's team. Gordon will move into a new race shop next season along with Johnson, who currently runs in the Busch series.

Jerry Nadeau and Terry Labonte, the other two drivers for Hendrick Motorsports, will remain in their current race shops.

"This is the future of Hendrick Motorsports, and I think you'll find it's the future of Winston Cup racing," Gordon said. "I think you'll see a lot more two-car teams working together like this, sharing information and building off each other."

Lowe's Home Improvement will sponsor the No. 48 Chevrolet Johnson will drive. The home improvement retailer is ending its sponsorship with Richard Childress Racing at the end of the year.

Mike Skinner, who currently drives the Lowe's sponsored car, is winless in five-plus seasons.

So, in introducing Johnson, who turned 26 Monday, the sponsor rolled out one of his new cars pulling a motorized ski craft.

"It may be a little small, but if you put that car into victory lane next year there will be a boat attached to it," said Bob Tillman, president of Lowe's.

Johnson, who has one win in the Busch series this season, will make his Winston Cup debut at Lowe's Motor Speedway next month. He'll also race in Homestead, Florida, and in Atlanta this year, then run a full schedule in 2002.

Johnson caught the eye of Gordon a few years ago during a test session at Darlington Raceway, when the three-time Winston Cup champion was surprised to see Johnson not shy away from rubbing the walls his first time out on NASCAR's most demanding track.

The two formed a friendship that eventually led Johnson to seek Gordon out for advice about his career. Gordon approached Hendrick about bringing Johnson aboard. The idea became a reality on Tuesday.

"Last year, when I had that talk with Jeff I thought what a great opportunity that would be, but will it come together?" Johnson said. "It has, and I couldn't be more excited. The fact that I get to drive for an organization like this and for someone like Jeff means so much to me."

GORDON MENTORS JOHNSON
Wednesday, October 10, 2001

Two weeks before his scheduled Winston Cup debut, Jimmie Johnson was called in for a meeting with the boss. For the next few hours, car owner Jeff Gordon explained the rigors of racing to Johnson, his hand-picked protégé.

There was one thing Gordon neglected to mention.

"I think what I forgot to talk to him about was just to keep that between the two of us," the three-time Winston Cup champion said. "I should have had that on my list."

Johnson's admission of the private meeting is just one of the many bumps the two are bound to have as Gordon crosses over to car owner and Johnson makes the move up to NASCAR's top series.

Although the two share good looks, charm and even humor, their careers couldn't be further apart.

At 30, Gordon has 58 career victories and is on the verge of winning his fourth Winston Cup title. He's got a lifetime contract at Hendrick Motorsports that makes him a partial owner in all its ventures, and is a savvy businessman.

Johnson, meanwhile, is 26 and by some standards getting a late start at the big time. He grew up racing motorcycles in Southern California and tried off-road racing before moving into stock cars in the American Speed Association.

He eventually made it to NASCAR's Busch series last season, and picked up his first career win three months ago. Although he's dreamed of Winston Cup racing, he's the first to admit he doesn't really have a clue what it's all about.

So how did they get together?

Perfect timing.

It was just over a year ago when Johnson, stuck in the Busch series and facing possible sponsor problems, had the good fortune to sit next to Gordon at a drivers' meeting. Needing advice on what his next career step should be, he gathered up the nerve to ask Gordon if they could talk.

"I was sort of surprised he even knew who I was, but he couldn't have been nicer and told me to come over to the truck and we'd talk," Johnson said. "I went in looking for advice and I walked out with the opportunity of a lifetime."

Unknown to Johnson, Gordon and team owner Rick Hendrick had talked just days earlier about finding a young driver for a fourth Hendrick team.

"He said 'This is just in the early stages, but we're looking for someone and I don't see why it couldn't be you,'" Johnson recalled. "I couldn't believe it, it was like a dream and I left there on cloud nine."

Not long after that, Johnson had a contract with Hendrick Motorsports and was ready to start the process of becoming a Winston Cup driver.

He's spent this season finishing out his Busch series contract and quietly watching Gordon to learn as much as he can. Once a sponsor was lined up, they decided to enter him in three Cup races this year to get some experience before a full schedule in 2002.

Johnson made his Winston Cup debut Sunday at Lowe's Motor Speedway, two weeks after Gordon's crash course preparing him for what to expect.

"To me, when you get to Winston Cup, it's so much bigger than life itself," Gordon said. "I came into it totally blind. I didn't have a clue how my life was going to change. ... If I had somebody to prepare me, I think it would have gotten me a few steps ahead at the beginning.

"So I thought it was important to talk to him about those things because I think what will bring Jimmie along even faster is to keep him well focused."

So Gordon has been mentoring Johnson about the demands he'll have on him on and off the track. He's talked to him about dealing with the media, how to handle overzealous fans, when to spend time away from the track and the importance of planning a schedule and sticking to it.

It all went exceptionally smooth last week, although it had the potential for disaster.

Johnson qualified 15th, five spots better than Gordon, who just laughed and shrugged at being shown up. He then counseled Johnson on the track and its grooves, cautioning him to stay out of trouble over the 500-mile race.

He didn't, though, and almost took Gordon with him when he spun out midway through the race. Gordon narrowly made it by, finishing 16th and retaining his lead in the points race.

Johnson finished 39th but didn't care. During the race, when he had moved up to fifth place, he radioed Gordon and the crew.

"Man, I'm living a dream out here," Johnson said.

He'll get two more starts this season, and probably much more advice from Gordon. Although Gordon swears he isn't planning on being a full-time car owner anytime soon, his affection and admiration for Johnson have him behaving differently.

"Jimmie is a heck of a talent, you put the right equipment under him and he's going to get it done," Gordon said. "He's going to be good enough pretty soon that I'll have to be careful and concentrate on just driving my own car."

SCHOOL OF HARD KNOCKS
Daytona Beach, Florida, Friday, February 15, 2002

There's not a lot of love flowing around the race track for Jimmie Johnson.

The rookie learned quickly that few veterans are hoping the polesitter wins Sunday's Daytona 500 and almost everyone wants to teach him a lesson.

He's been bumped, banged, pushed out of the draft, toyed into making a move at the wrong time and basically treated like a pesky little kid. Never mind that the 26-year-old Johnson drives for Hendrick Motorsports and four-time Winston Cup champion Jeff Gordon.

"He's been schooled out there a few times," crew chief Chad Knaus said. "I see some of the guys setting him up, getting ready to put a move on him, and I just let it happen. Jimmie needs to figure out the tendencies of these guys or else it will keep happening."

This isn't how Johnson dreamed his first Daytona 500 would be. Never did he expect to have the fastest car out of the gate, dominating the first few rounds of practice and winning the pole for the season-opening race.

He took little time to celebrate because he knew the good times weren't going to last.

The day after he took the pole, no one wanted to work with Johnson on the track.

Tony Stewart set him up, pretending to go one way on a passing attempt then blowing by Johnson the other way as Johnson found himself in the wrong spot to try a block.

Ward Burton has pushed him out of the draft, and Dale Jarrett also led Johnson astray during a practice.

"That first day after I won the pole, I think I was hung out 20 times," Johnson said. "It was pretty humbling. All I could do was go home and think about it, try to figure out what I did wrong. It made it a little hard to sleep."

He didn't give up and was much better the next day. He still made mistakes, but was only kicked out of line two times. And he started to figure out whom he could trust on the race track and whom he should avoid.

In theory, he should be able to trust Gordon and his other two teammates, Terry Labonte and Jerry Nadeau. But in the biggest race of the year, it's every man for himself.

"First you need your teammates around you, then you have to hope you're better," Johnson said. "Because if they've got the run, they aren't going to wait around for you."

That happened to him in Thursday's first qualifying race, when Gordon passed Johnson in Turn 1 of the first lap of the race and didn't stick around to make sure Johnson could keep up.

Johnson got shuffled back, and in trying to get move up, drove below the yellow line on the race track. He tried to slow up to avoid coming back over the line ahead of the car next to him - improving position while under the line is against the rules - but Burton bumped him from behind.

Unable to slow or risk a wreck, he motored forward, passed the car next to him and got slapped with a stop-and-go penalty. It put him so far out of the race that had Johnson not already won the pole in time trials, he would not have qualified for the 500.

"I was a little bummed about that race," Johnson said.

"But I just chalk it up as another learning experience and try to take something from it into Sunday's race. There's not much else you can do."

JOHNSON'S FIRST WINSTON CUP VICTORY
Fontana, California, Monday, April 29, 2002

Jimmie Johnson's parents watched their son's first Winston Cup victory on TV from their home in Concord, North Carolina.

Rick Hendrick and Jeff Gordon, co-owners of the rookie's car, were at California Speedway and acting like proud parents. Their protégé held off Kurt Busch on Sunday to win the NAPA Auto Parts 500 in only his 13th Winston Cup start.

"Jeff and I thought he was such a good talent," said Hendrick, whose team also fields Chevrolets for Gordon, Terry Labonte and Jerry Nadeau. "He didn't have a sponsor, didn't know what the team was going to look like. We just knew he was a young boy with a lot of talent."

Hendrick also brought Gordon, now a four-time series champion and winner of 58 races, to NASCAR's top stock car series.

"When you see them, you just try to take advantage of it," he said. "I never dreamed we'd do this well this quick."

Gordon lost a lap because of an unscheduled pit stop and finished 16th. This was the 18th race in a row without a victory for the defending series champ.

Still, he trotted breathlessly to the victory celebration.

"I didn't know that Jimmie had won," Gordon said. "I went from being real mad about my day to being really happy and excited for Jimmie."

Once he realized Johnson had won, Gordon pulled alongside to bump the side of the No. 48 Chevy in salute and give a big thumbs-up.

"When the right chemistry gets put together, it doesn't matter how many races you've got under your belt," Gordon said.

Johnson, whose previous best was third last month in Atlanta, admitted he was surprised to win so soon.

"Heck, yeah," he said. "You always think you've got enough ability to win, but you never know until you get out there and do it."

Johnson was so excited he overdid the celebration, smoking his tires and spinning the car on the track and through the grass until he blew the engine and transmission.

Johnson lived in El Cajon, about 100 miles from the track, before his family moved to North Carolina.

"This is unbelievable," he said. "I know my mom and dad are sitting at home going crazy and wishing they were here."

Johnson beat Busch by about six car-lengths on the 2-mile oval. Much of the credit goes to crew chief Chad Knaus, who gambled on a fuel-only pit stop near the end. Knaus earned his first win in only his second full season as a crew chief.

"It paid off," he said. "I was going to get sick to my stomach and throw up after I made the call, but it worked out well."

His driver didn't question the gamble.

"I smiled because I knew what it was going to do for us," Johnson said. "It was going to put us out in front. I was just hoping that Kurt wasn't going to do the same thing."

Busch had the best car in the first half of the 250-lap race, building a lead of 15 seconds before a caution flag on lap 141 tightened the race.

After that, it was a battle among Busch, former series champion Dale Jarrett, Ricky Rudd and Johnson.

Jarrett was out front on lap 229 when Kevin Harvick and Dale Earnhardt Jr. wrecked in the fourth turn, bringing out the final caution.

The left rear tire on Harvick's car blew as he raced through turn three. As the car veered down the banked track, Earnhardt's car slammed into the driver side, sending both into the concrete wall.

Harvick was not injured, but Earnhardt bruised his right ankle and left the infield medical center on crutches. He was to have the swollen ankle checked Monday in North Carolina.

Most of the lead lap cars took advantage of the caution to pit, but Bill Elliott stayed on the track and was just ahead of Johnson for the restart on lap 237. Johnson's car shot past Elliott's Dodge in the first turn and stayed out front.

Busch, driving a Ford, moved past Elliott and Rudd and grabbed the runner-up spot on lap 247. He couldn't catch Johnson, who crossed the finish line 0.620 seconds ahead.

Rudd was third, followed by Elliott, Busch's teammate Mark Martin, Jarrett, series leader Sterling Marlin and 2001 California winner Rusty Wallace.

Busch wore a straw hat after the race in honor of team owner Jack Roush, who is recovering from an April 19 plane crash. Busch could hardly believe Johnson beat him without taking tires.

"You never expect to get beat by fuel only," he said. "We just didn't have the right position at the right time."

ROOKIE JOHNSON WINS AT DOVER
Dover, Delaware, Monday, June 3, 2002

Jimmie Johnson established his target long ago, and becoming rookie of the year now seems easily within his grasp.

On Sunday, he won for the second time this season and was asked about an even bigger prize - the Winston Cup championship.

"We've got a shot at it," said Johnson, second in the series standings after his victory at Dover International Speedway. "Is it realistic? I don't think so, but crazy things happen."

No rookie has won the title, and Johnson is a long way from pressing leader Sterling Marlin, who holds a 136-point edge after 13 of 36 races.

So despite a level of success surpassed by only one rookie - Tony Stewart, who won three times in 1999 - Johnson thinks there will be difficult moments ahead.

"I guess we might be a dark horse if we were to be anything," Johnson said. "But if we keep finishing races, it will take care of itself."

Rookie NASCAR driver Jimmie Johnson, center, races his Lowes Ford through the third turn during the Pocono 500 at the Pocono Raceway in Long Pond, Pennsylvania, June 9, 2002. (AP Photo/Chris Gardner)

Marlin will have to help with a few poor runs, but he's been extremely efficient all season, avoiding horrible, points-robbing finishes. He's also been getting a few breaks, like the problems that cost Matt Kenseth and Mark Martin a chance to advance when Marlin finished 13th in the MBNA Platinum 400.

Kenseth wound up 40th and Martin 41st, replaced in the second and third positions by Johnson and Jeff Gordon. It was a net gain of 49 points for Marlin. But he was not entirely satisfied.

"We gained a lot of points," Marlin said. "But we want to win."

He's done that twice this season, and decent finishes the rest of the way could give him his first title.

Still, Marlin's nearest pursuer is a rookie, and Johnson was asked how he would handle the pressure should he be close to the leader late in the season.

"I'm not going to pay too much attention to it," Johnson said. "There have been certain times during my career that I've faced pressure, and I've gotten used to it. I've found a way to deal with it relatively well."

He did just that Sunday, redeeming himself for errors that probably cost him a victory a week earlier.

Despite dominating the middle part of the race, Johnson was 10th after most of the contenders stopped for gas with 92 of 400 laps remaining.

"At that point I thought, 'Let's just get a top five,'" Johnson explained. "I was just trying to pass everybody in front of me, and there was the 28, and I said, 'We made it.'"

Johnson passed four-time Dover winner Ricky Rudd to take the lead on lap 363. Then, Johnson remained on the track when a final caution waved for Ken Schrader's blown rear end with 28 laps left.

"Track position was everything," Johnson said.

The others pitted for tires in hopes of catching Johnson, but he drove away in his Chevrolet on the restart and beat the Dodge of four-time Dover winner Bill Elliott by a half-second.

"I didn't realize Elliott was coming that hard, and I had to step it back up to stay up there," Johnson said. "These guys gave me a great race car."

He deserved it, said Chad Knaus, crew chief of the car owned by Gordon and Hendrick Motorsports.

"I've got the best driver in Winston Cup, the best crew and the best car owner," Knaus said.

Johnson began to take command when he passed leader Gordon on the 144th lap.

Johnson also had the strongest car last week in the Coca-Cola 600, but lost after making mistakes - including overshooting his pit stall - late in the race. Last month, he threw away another chance by crashing in the waning laps.

"I did not blow it like I did in Richmond and Charlotte," said Johnson, who joined the late Davey Allison (1987) as the only rookie winner in Dover's 33 years of racing.

It was Johnson's Winston Cup debut on The Monster Mile, one of the most difficult tracks on the NASCAR circuit - where his boss won for the fourth time last June. This time, the 30-year Gordon, a four-time series champion, was no match for his 26-year-old protégé.

Third was Jeff Burton, followed by Ryan Newman and Dale Jarrett. All were in Fords.

HENDRICK MOTORSPORTS THE TEAM TO BEAT
Wednesday, August 25, 2004

Once considered misguided for building a multicar team, Rick Hendrick's idea has become the model for successful teams in NASCAR's top series. And now, after a few seasons of struggle, Hendrick Motorsports is again the team to beat.

The head of one of the country's biggest automotive groups, Hendrick has had his share of success outside and inside racing. He's a wealthy, successful man, and his team has won a total of 126 races and five Cup championships since it was begun in 1984 with a one-car entry for Geoff Bodine.

Now he has a four-car team - once thought to be a revolutionary and unworkable idea.

Going into Saturday night's race at Bristol, Hendrick drivers Jeff Gordon and Jimmie Johnson are 1-2 in the season standings and very much in contention for another series title, while Terry Labonte is 23rd and rookie Brian Vickers 24th.

Multicar teams weren't a very popular concept when Hendrick came into the sport. Two cars on a single team were generally considered one too many.

But Hendrick saw it differently, running cars for Bodine and Tim Richmond in 1986, making it three cars in 1988 with Bodine, Darrell Waltrip and Ken Schrader and, finally, escalating to four entries in 2002 with Gordon, Johnson, Labonte and Joe Nemechek.

"It didn't work out overnight," acknowledged Hendrick, whose team won races but no championships until the '90's. "A lot of people told me, 'You can't do that. The drivers and crew chiefs won't share what they know and it will cause problems.' But I was pretty confident we had the right approach."

When Hendrick offered a ride to then-struggling former series champion Terry Labonte in 1994, he gladly accepted the opportunity despite the many naysayers.

"I remember when I joined the team, everybody said, 'Oh man, you're making a mistake. You shouldn't go down there. That's not going to work,'" said Labonte, who joined Gordon and Schrader on the Hendrick team.

"After I went down there and saw how he did things, I was real impressed," Labonte added. "And now it's the opposite. Everybody says if you don't have a multicar team, you might as well stay home. The multicar team gives you more information, better ideas and the opportunity to do a variety of things."

Things really came together for the team in the '90's.

Gordon, who joined the Hendrick team as a rookie in 1993, gave the owner his first series title in 1995. Labonte beat him for the championship in 1996, but Gordon added two more in 1997 and 1998 - the only time in history a team has won four straight titles in NASCAR's premier series. Gordon won a fourth crown in 2001.

Along with adding drivers, the overall Hendrick Motorsports acreage and payroll have grown enormously, with more than 400 employees spread across a complex of buildings on 70 acres in suburban Charlotte, N.C.

And as big as the team has gotten, there is still an atmosphere of togetherness that is rare in such a big organization.

"Rick just brings you into his family, and that's rare and unique," Johnson said. "He gives everybody on the complex the things they need to have the best performance possible.

"So when you come into a situation like that, where his No. 1 focus is to win races and championships, and then you have that environment where you're part of a family, it's the greatest place in the world to be."

Still, winning only one title in the past five years hasn't been very fulfilling for anybody at Hendrick Motorsports.

The team owner still thinks the key to getting back on top, though, is working together as a team and sharing information.

"I think we started rebuilding back in 2000," Hendrick said. "We told everyone at a (preseason) media tour, 'We're going to win together, and we're going to lose together, but we're going to be together.'

"And every crew chief and every driver that's come into the organization since then, and everybody that's been involved in a management-type position, we've had the goal of working together, sharing information and making it work."

Hendrick's concept seems to be working just fine.

Although Johnson is slumping right now, failing to finish three straight races and losing the points lead to his teammate, and while Gordon has struggled at times this season, those two will definitely be among the favorites when NASCAR's new 10-race showdown for the Nextel Cup begins next month.

"Everybody talks about it, but our guys really do work together," Hendrick said. "The chemistry on this team's the best I've ever had in 20 years - at least the 18 that I've run multiple cars.

"And I think that's paying off for us."

JIMMIE JOHNSON WINS 2ND CHAMPIONSHIP
Homestead, Florida, Monday, November 19, 2007

After 10 months, 36 races and endless questions about defending his Nextel Cup championship, Jimmie Johnson could finally relax.

"South Beach, here we come," said Johnson, who promised to "watch the sun come up and smile."

Another title was his, and he was going to savor it, too.

Johnson became the first driver to win consecutive championships since Jeff Gordon in 1997 and '98, wrapping up the title by finishing a trouble-free seventh in the season finale at Homestead-Miami Speedway. Matt Kenseth won the race.

When it was over, Johnson and crew chief Chad Knaus were already thinking about a third.

"We're just really hitting our stride," Johnson said. "I think that we have a lot of good years ahead of us and we'll be fighting for more championships and certainly winning more races as the years go by, and hopefully be a three-time champion in the near future."

This Sunday drive was a coronation, and Johnson knew it. Deep down, so did everyone else, too. NASCAR is changing eras next season, but the Johnson era atop the sport is just getting started.

Team owner Rick Hendrick was along for the ride when Gordon ruled the sport, and said it's clear this is Johnson's time now.

"Jimmie's just getting better and better, phenomenal," Hendrick said. "He's as determined as anybody I've ever seen sit down in a race car. I don't see anything that's going to slow Jimmie down. I hope that we can keep it together. We can do some phenomenal things in the future.

Jimmie Johnson, center, celebrates after winning the NASCAR Nextel Cup Series championship in Homestead, Florida. NASCAR CEO Brian France is on the right, and Nextel chief marketing officer Tim Kelly is on the left, November 18, 2007. (AP Photo/Alan Diaz)

"Can we get 10, guys?" Hendrick asked, looking at Johnson and Knaus. "OK, we're going to get 10."

Johnson came into the event with a cushy 86-point lead over Gordon, his friend, mentor and teammate at Hendrick Motorsports. Although Johnson only needed to finish 18th or better, he refused to play it safe and Knaus gave him a pole-winning car.

Johnson led the first lap to earn a quick five-point bonus, then settled in for the 400-mile ride into the record books. At a time when no single team is supposed to dominate, the No. 48 crew did just that in leading Johnson to 10 victories and a stout 5.0 average finish during the Chase for the championship.

It put it out of reach for Gordon, who was hoping to add a fifth Cup title to his dream season. He became a father in June, won six races and his fourth-place finish Sunday was his NASCAR-record 30th top-10 finish of the year.

"It's an awesome year, but you know what? We wanted to win a championship and we got beat," said Gordon, who pulled alongside Johnson for a celebratory nudge and pumped his fist in excitement during Johnson's burnout.

Gordon was also terrific in the Chase, winning twice and averaging a 5.1 finish. Yet it wasn't enough against Johnson, his handpicked teammate who wound up surpassing him as the sport's dominant driver.

Johnson became the first driver since Gordon to win double-digit races, four in a row and the consecutive titles. His 77-point victory margin was the largest in the four years of the Chase.

"I'll be honest, I really thought that as aggressive as they were being, it was going to bite them," Gordon said. "I guess I was just a little bit too confident in the old consistency thing. ... Man, if they didn't pull it off. That's how good they are."

It was a far different approach from last year, when Johnson fretted over everything, especially the outcome. He had lost the championship in 2004 and 2005, and the stress of it made him unable to relax.

"Losing those two championships taught us a lot. It was painful," Johnson said. "And there were points there where we went back, looked at it and tried to adjust. And it's led to these two championships."

Finally winning last year chilled him out, and the California kid had a "no worries" attitude during the entire Chase. He packed a quick trip to Mexico into his schedule two weeks ago, spent time hanging out in New York City and even made plans for his championship party a week in advance.

"After what I experienced last season and coming into this season, and even this night, it just went so much smoother for me," he said. "I was in the right frame of mind, was focused on the right things. I had great support from the crew guys, great support from my loving wife and everything came together. We're rocking."

The attitude was infectious for the entire team.

Before the Super Bowl in South Florida nine months ago, Colts quarterback Peyton Manning said he slept for 12 hours the night before the game, and knew that was a good sign.

Same thing here. This was Johnson's Super Bowl, and his team couldn't have been more relaxed.

Knaus the sort of guy who frets over every detail went to bed at 9 p.m. Saturday, awoke at 8 a.m. and couldn't have been calmer when he got to the track a couple hours later.

"I've got the best team and the best driver," Knaus said.

Who can argue? Certainly not NASCAR.

"He is having a run that in the modern era is maybe unmatched," NASCAR chairman Brian France said before the race. "He is just at a different level and I think it's hats off to him."

The sport has come a long way from the days when Richard Petty won 27 races in a season, and too many teams are competitive for any one driver to dominate. But Hendrick Motorsports did it, with its four drivers winning 18 of the 36 races and Johnson taking the lion's share while giving HMS its seventh Cup championship.

It came in a season when NASCAR phased in its Car of Tomorrow, a safer, cost-efficient car that was also designed to improve the racing. But teams had to flop back and forth between the current car and the CoT, and mastering both programs was a chore.

Sunday's finale was the last race for the current car, as a new era begins next season when NASCAR will use the CoT exclusively. The series name also is changing, from Nextel Cup to Sprint Cup.

And the dynamic at Hendrick also will be different, with Dale Earnhardt Jr. NASCAR's most popular driver set to replace the temperamental Kyle Busch on the four-car team. The addition will give Hendrick another championship-caliber driver and a colorful personality on a team often criticized for being a bit bland.

It's stretched to Johnson, who despite his success isn't embraced by a fan base that views him as a little too polished and a lot too nice. He proved he's not perfect last December, falling from the top of a golf cart and breaking his wrist in the process. Embarrassed by the incident and afraid of what it would do to his image, he initially lied about how it happened and was angry when the truth came out.

When it didn't harm him, Johnson realized he doesn't always have to be the consummate corporate poster boy and can show his wild side.

He did just that when he crossed the finish line Sunday, immediately radioing to his crew to get ready for the party.

Chapter 3

FADING COMPETITIVENESS

NASCAR driver Jeff Gordon prepares to depart the garage during practice for the Bank of America 500 auto race at the Lowe's Motor Speedway in Concord, North Carolina, October 13, 2006. (AP Photo/Gerry Broome)

LONGEST CAREER DROUGHT
Kansas City, Kansas, Wednesday, May 8, 2002

If this is a slump, Jeff Gordon will take it. So would most of the other drivers on NASCAR's Winston Cup circuit.

Since winning the Protection One 400 last September 30 at Kansas Speedway, the defending Cup champion hasn't won in 19 races. That's the longest drought of a career, now in its 10th year, that has seen Gordon win four Cup titles and more than $47 million.

But he's still in sixth place, only 25 points out of a tie for third - and not doing too badly as a first-year owner, either.

"You talk about Jeff being in a 'slump'," said John Andretti, who is 35th in the standings headed into a rare two-week break in the Winston Cup schedule. "There are a lot of guys who would like to be in Jeff's 'slump'."

Gordon, who came to Kansas City, Kansas, with Andretti and Jimmy Spencer to test tires for Goodyear on Tuesday and Wednesday, said Wednesday that his six-win championship season in 2001 fueled fans' expectations of similar success this year.

"We did a lot of great things last year," he said. "Coming into this season, we kind of expected to keep on rolling, but this sport will humble you in a hurry."

Gordon wouldn't use the word "slump" to describe his season in the No. 24 Chevrolet so far. He has six Top 10 finishes - two in the top five - in 11 races, including a second-place finish on April 8 in the Samsung/Radio Shack 500 at Texas Motor Speedway.

None of his top 10 finishes has come after a start on the inside front, though. Gordon won the poles for the Food City 500 and Virginia 500 but finished 31st and 23rd, respectively.

"I recognize how competitive the sport is," he said. "You'll go along at times and win races and say, 'How the heck did we do that? We didn't do anything different.' Then you'll go along and not win races and say, 'We aren't doing anything different; why aren't we winning?'"

Gordon announced on March 16 that his wife, Brooke, had filed for divorce - but since then, he has refused to blame the upheaval in his personal life for his failure to win on the track.

The encouraging thing, he said Wednesday, is that he has been in contention in a number of races.

"Daytona, we had a shot at winning. We had great cars at Darlington ... and Martinsville and got caught up in wrecks, running first or second," he said. "Those are tough to take, but at the same time I'd rather get caught in something like that running up front battling for a win, than running at the back of the pack and struggling."

Speaking of packs, just seven points behind Gordon in the Cup standings is rookie Jimmie Johnson, whose No. 48 Chevrolet is co-owned by Gordon and Rick Hendrick.

Johnson has two poles and seven top-10 finishes this year, including his first win on April 28 in the NAPA 500 at California Speedway.

"It's been interesting to see Jimmie come along, and that crew," Gordon said. "It's exciting to see them get a win."

The relationship between Johnson and crew chief Chad Knaus is one reason for the rookie's quick rise into the Top 10, Gordon said.

"Chad and Jimmie have really jelled right away," he said. "That's something that has to happen on its own, or it doesn't happen. Jimmie and Chad, they're both like sponges. They just absorb all this information, and they're open to whatever you tell them."

DROUGHT ENDS
Bristol, Tennessee, Sunday, August 25, 2002

Jeff Gordon hoisted the enormous Bristol Motor Speedway trophy over his head, hesitant to ever put it down.

It had been so long since he last stood in Victory Lane - confetti raining down on him, fireworks popping above - that Gordon wanted to savor every moment of this win.

"It feels like the first one all over again," Gordon said after bumping his way past Rusty Wallace to win the Sharpie 500 on Saturday night and snap his 31-race winless streak.

"I can tell you, we do not take wins for granted. These things are hard to come by and we appreciate them. That moment there in Victory Lane, I wanted to pause it and burn it into my memory forever because it's just such an awesome, awesome feeling."

For the first 23 races of this season, all Gordon felt was mounting frustration over his inability to get in front and stay there. There were weeks when the Hendrick Motorsports team gave him great cars, but driver error sabotaged their efforts.

And there were weeks when the No. 24 Chevrolet was simply junk, unable to even sniff the front of the pack. Races like these left the entire team wondering what had gone so wrong since Gordon wrapped up his fourth Winston Cup championship last November.

For a driver and a team used to dominance - he now has 59 victories in a career that has included 10- and 13-win seasons - not winning since September 30, 2001 was absolute agony.

"When you go as long as we've gone without a win and you realize just how hard it is and how hard you work for them, and just how everything's got to fall in place to get there, you look back and go, 'How in the world did we win 58 races?'" Gordon said.

Jeff Gordon runs during qualifying for the NASCAR Sharpie 500 at Bristol Motor Speedway. Gordon took the pole position for Saturday's race with a speed of 124.034 mph,
Aug. 23, 2002. (AP Photo/John Russell)

Well, he won 47 of them with Ray Evernham as his crew chief
and the original "Rainbow Warriors" servicing his cars. But Evernham split midway through the 1999 season to become a car owner,
and the Warriors also branched out.

So Gordon had to adjust to new crew chief Robbie Loomis' style
and a new crew. It took some time, but they broke through last season with six victories and the Winston Cup title.

Then everything hit a snag, personally and professionally.

First Gordon struggled on the track, then his wife, Brooke, filed
for divorce after seven years of marriage in March. For years, they
were the most dashing couple in NASCAR.

So the 31-year-old Gordon has been going it alone this season,
performing a delicate balancing act of figuring out who he is while
trying to focus on his job. As the winless streak dragged into the
summer, it became difficult for Gordon to convince his critics that
his pending divorce wasn't a distraction.

He swears he never lost his focus but admits he sometimes wondered what was wrong with him.

"You go through times when you work just as hard and are doing everything the same, and it's just not happening," he said. "You just start to question a lot of things, but my confidence in my driving, I don't think that I ever really questioned that."

He knew the only thing that could make him happy was a victory, and he wanted that badly.

So Gordon went to Bristol, where he had four career victories but none in the prestigious Saturday night race. He was sure he could get one. He broke a six-race qualifying slump by earning the pole, then led a race-high 235 laps.

But Wallace seemed in control in the waning laps until lapped traffic slowed him and gave Gordon a chance to steal the win. He did it with three laps left in the race, tapping Wallace's Ford enough to knock him out of his way and coast on by.

Wallace, riding his own 50-race winless streak, was furious and plotted his revenge. But lapped traffic made it impossible for him to catch Gordon and bump him back.

"I tried desperately to knock the heck out of him, I just couldn't catch him," Wallace said. "It's been a long time since I've won. I guess my day is coming, but, man, I tried real hard."

It was similar to another bump-and-run Gordon put on Wallace to win the spring race at Bristol in 1997. Gordon has no regrets over either episode. With a chance to break his streak, he was going for it.

"If he wants to pay me back, if that's the way he wants to go about it, I've been knocked around, I've been moved out of the way, and I've been wrecked," he said. "I go to the next race, focus on what I've got to do, not taking guys out and doing paybacks.

"He's going to be upset. He lost the race and he wanted it as bad as I did. I don't expect him to be happy. We may talk, we may not talk. We'll just kind of go to Darlington and see what happens. But I'm not calling him."

STILL A TITLE THREAT
Darlington, South Carolina, Wednesday, August 28, 2002

Through six months of losing, Jeff Gordon was routinely asked when he'd finally win a race. His answer was always the same: Winning races is great, but championships are even better.

Now that Gordon has snapped his 31-race winless streak - breaking through by bumping Rusty Wallace out of his way to win at Bristol Motor Speedway last weekend - the attention has shifted to his bid for a fifth Winston Cup title.

"Never have we counted ourselves out of it," Gordon said. "We just knew that if we were going to be a threat, we had to start performing. Hopefully, (the Bristol win) is the first step to that."

Actually, Gordon was never out of the points chase this season. Although he had repeatedly failed to make it to the winner's circle, his knack for keeping the No. 24 Chevrolet on the track had kept him in the title hunt.

Heading into the Southern 500, Gordon has been running at the end of 55-straight races, a modern-day NASCAR record. The consistency had kept him in the top five of the points standings, and his victory at Bristol pulled him into third place, 111 points behind leader Sterling Marlin.

That's got to be a little too close for comfort to the challengers trying to prevent him from repeating as Winston Cup champion.

And it doesn't help the field that they are headed to Darlington Raceway, one of the many tracks Gordon has conquered.

He's got five wins here - including a record four-straight Southern 500 victories from 1995-98 - finished in the top 10 in 13 of the 19 races he's competed in and led more than 1,100 laps. His lowest finish was a 40th in March 2001, when he failed to finish the race because of engine failure.

That was his last DNF, which started his record-streak and helped him stay positive during the 11 months between victories. Before Bristol, his last win was September 30, 2001.

"When we weren't winning, finishing the races is what kept us in the points chase," Gordon said. "Consistency wins championships and we stayed within striking distance during our winless streak."

It certainly wasn't easy - not with the mounting pressure and increased attention the streak brought.

At every single race track this season, Gordon would take his customary spot on the top step of his hauler and face the media. Without fail, someone would always ask, "Is this the week you'll break your streak?"

Crew chief Robbie Loomis said Gordon's ability to stand up to the scrutiny helped the Hendrick Motorsports team keep plugging away.

"Jeff Gordon has really been the glue that's held us together," Loomis said. "The confidence Jeff has, because he's won so many championships, provides a calming effect on the rest of us. The little things Jeff would say kept us going in the right direction."

Sometimes it was what he didn't say that helped.

There were times Gordon could have pointed fingers at his team, demanding to know why his car couldn't get to the front - especially at tracks where he'd always had success.

Although driver error had certainly played its part in the losing, there were plenty of weeks when his car was pure junk and he was never a factor. But Gordon kept the team together instead of tearing it apart by blaming others.

"Jeff has really been the one all year who's been the calmest, the one who calms the waters and soothes us," Loomis aid. "Whether it would be a bad practice or a bad race, he would say, 'Hey, we've been on this streak, and everybody is freaking out.'

"Well, I was freaking out, but he kept us looking at that goal of what we were working toward, and that kind of calmed us for a little bit."

So Gordon was the team cheerleader, a much different role then what he had played in years past.

But everything about this year is different.

He's going through a high-profile divorce after seven years of marriage and his bid to live his life as a single man has been just as public.

After spending his first nine years in Winston Cup as somewhat of a recluse, preferring quiet nights with his wife over bonding sessions with the guys, Gordon is now venturing out of the motorhome lot more and more on race weekends.

He can suddenly be found playing video games or go-karting with other drivers, grabbing a burger with some old buddies, even walking around the crowded pits at the local dirt tracks, where he mingles with the up-and-coming drivers and signs autographs for the fans.

He organized a charity bowling tournament earlier this month in Indianapolis that drew only A-List racing celebrities, and afterward, he grabbed a group and headed out for a night on the town.

It's hardly been the behavior of a driver lamenting a recent run of bad breaks and personal problems.

Maybe that's because Gordon never gave up, knowing that sooner or later, confidence and hard work would have him back in the winner's circle. And when that happened, everyone would know that Gordon was coming - racing toward a fifth title.

"As far as the championship, I think it serves notice to a lot of people that we're not out of it," Gordon said. "I'm not saying that now we're going to run away with it, we've still got a lot of hard work ahead of us. But (the win) is going to do so much for the team morale, and sometimes morale and attitude can take you up several notches performance-wise."

BACK IN THE HUNT
Charlotte, North Carolina, Wednesday, October 22, 2003

A shot at a fifth Winston Cup title slipped away from Jeff Gordon in July when poor pit strategy ruined his race in New Hampshire. The eight-race slide that followed sent him plummeting in the points standings.

He was a mere afterthought by late September, forced to defend the strength of his team and reiterate his confidence in his crew chief.

Down but never really out, a late-season surge has Gordon back on the winning track.

Gordon won his second race of the season last week, and a string of five consecutive top five finishes has put him within striking distance of second place in the standings. He's still in sixth place, but trails Kevin Harvick for second by just 106 points with four races remaining.

"I really hate that we had that August and part of September like we did," Gordon said. "I'd love to be up there battling for that championship, but that kind of took us back a little bit. We're just fighting back as hard as we can to win races and finish the season on a positive note."

The slide began in July, when Gordon led a race-high 133 laps in New Hampshire only to finish 24th after a gamble on pit road backfired. He left the track at an all-time emotional low, all too aware that his chase for the championship had just taken a substantial hit.

"I'm just so devastated in our own performance right now," he said as he wearily exited the track that day. "I'm completely in shock and I'm just completely drained from the devastation."

Things only got worse from there. He started from the pole in New Hampshire in August, but was spun out on the first lap, then battled back into second before getting spun out again as he headed to the finish line low on gas. He finished 33rd.

A mechanical problem the next week left him 30th, he started from the pole the following week in Bristol only to wreck and finish 28th, and an accident with Casey Mears left him 32nd in the Southern 500.

By his second trip to New Hampshire in September - when he spun out on pit road and hit some of teammate Jimmie Johnson's crew members - Gordon was in the middle of a full slump and had slipped to a season-low sixth in the standings.

Frustration for the No. 24 team was at an all-time low. But Gordon, who dealt with a divorce while struggling through a 31-race winless streak last season, fought through it.

"As a teammate and a friend, I can tell you he doesn't get rattled by much," Johnson said. "By everything we've seen with his personal life and his career, you can't get inside his head and that's one of the big strengths Jeff Gordon has."

So Gordon forged ahead, confirming his support for crew chief Robbie Loomis.

Despite guiding Gordon to his fourth Winston Cup title in 2001, Loomis has struggled to build the steady consistency Gordon was known for while winning his first three championships.

When the questions started coming about his confidence in Loomis' leadership, Gordon laughed.

"It's just ridiculous," he said. "I'm thrilled with Robbie being in there."

The duo has even turned it around.

Gordon has led a series-high 1,580 laps this year and last week continued his streak of 10 consecutive seasons with multiple victories. The victory at Martinsville (Virginia) Speedway took away any pressure the team had been under, and allowed Gordon and his crew to relax as they head into the final month of the season.

"It was awesome to see the look on Robbie's face and the guys on the team and how excited they were," Gordon said. "You can have all the pep talks in the world and pat one another on the back and you can even pay them a bunch of money, and nothing is like getting to Victory Lane."

ON VERGE OF RETURNING TO VICTORY LANE
Charlotte, North Carolina, Monday, February 23, 2009

Rick Hendrick began his 25th season in NASCAR full of expectations for his storied organization.

He predicted newcomer Mark Martin would make all four of his drivers championship contenders, that Dale Earnhardt Jr. would find a comfort level at Hendrick Motorsports and Jimmie Johnson would continue his run through the NASCAR record books.

But for Jeff Gordon, his 17-year money man, the boss had a promise: Gordon would win again.

"Multiple races," Hendrick insisted. "No doubt about it."

So far, Gordon is 0-for-2. But the first two races suggest he'll be back in Victory Lane very soon.

Gordon led 64 laps Sunday night before finishing second at Auto Club Speedway. The four-time series champion was unable to chase down winner Matt Kenseth over the closing laps, but he found some consolation: His No. 24 team is far ahead of where it was this time last year, when Gordon had his first winless season since his 1993 rookie campaign.

"I'm so excited about this race team right now," he said. "I just think we're head and shoulders above where we were. I know it's just a couple races in, and this is one race. I love the way the car was driving."

He couldn't say that often last year, when he was slow to adjust to NASCAR's full-time use of its new model car. Although he was third at Fontana a year ago, and notched three top-10 finishes through the first six races, it wasn't a true indication of where the team was in terms of preparation or performance.

It became evident in April, when a crash caused him to finish last in Texas, and he followed with nondescript runs in Phoenix and Talladega. As the season wore on, the results that once had come so easily never materialized.

Soon it was October and he was at Lowe's Motor Speedway, a year removed from the last of his 81 victories. His fans were adamant that crew chief Steve Letarte was the problem. Gordon refused to cast blame, especially against someone who had guided him to a NASCAR-record 30 top-10 finishes in 36 starts just one year before. But, as his chances to return to Victory Lane dwindled, nothing seemed to change.

Hendrick believes Gordon's struggles last season were a companywide failure to provide the driver with the right tools.

"We were just not good enough for that team. I think Jeff is so used to carrying it on his shoulders, I think we all just gave up at one point there, but it motivated us to come back," Hendrick said. "That was the first year, I feel like we just let him down."

Gordon, however, takes responsibility. His back had been bothering him since his failed 2007 title run, and he never seriously considered a treatment for the spasms and tightness that sometimes broke his concentration in the car. He also admits his adjustment to the new car was slow despite one of his most extensive testing schedules.

Some drivers coming off such a year might question how much longer they can race. Gordon used it to refire his passion and rebuild his commitment to winning.

His wife, Ingrid, persuaded him to start a legitimate fitness routine, use a personal trainer and hire someone at the track to help him prepare his back for the rigors of 500 miles of racing.

And Letarte wanted an overhaul, handing Hendrick a list of changes he needed following the season finale at Homestead. He altered the engineering group, tinkered with personnel and the cars themselves.

The result was his win in a Daytona 500 qualifying race, Gordon's first trip to Victory Lane in almost 16 months. But it didn't count at least not for not points and he's focused on snapping his 43-race winless streak.

He led 14 laps in the season-opening Daytona 500, but was 13th when rain halted the race and Kenseth was declared the winner. Had it gone the distance, Gordon is certain he would have contended for the win. And if he had a few more miles Sunday, he wonders if he would have run down Kenseth.

Regardless, he's positive he'll soon make Hendrick look like a prophet.

"I just feel good when I get in the car," he said. "The car is driving good. It's just starting off right. I think we only have room for improvement."

Chapter 4

BATTLES FOUGHT

Start of the race in turn four of the Aaron's 499 at Talladega Superspeedway, Talladega, Alabama, April 25, 2004. (AP Photo/Kevin Glackmeyer)

WIN OVER EARNHARDT AT TALLADEGA
Talladega, Alabama, Sunday, April 25, 2004

This time, the decision went Jeff Gordon's way.

After a NASCAR ruling went against him a week earlier in Martinsville, Virginia, costing Gordon a shot at victory, the sanctioning organization handed the four-time Nextel Cup champion a controversial win Sunday at Talladega Super-speedway.

Gordon seized the lead from Dale Earnhardt Jr. with six laps remaining and barely beat him, ending DEI's winning streak at Talladega and bringing a rain of beer cans and garbage from the pro-Earnhardt fans.

"I don't mind a little controversy, especially when it goes my way," Gordon said, smiling.

In Martinsville, Gordon had little to smile about after his car was damaged when he hit a large piece of concrete that had dislodged from the track while running second. NASCAR refused to let Gordon's Hendrick Motorsports team repair the car during the 77-minute delay while the track was being repaired. He wound up sixth.

Sunday, with Earnhardt making a strong move to pass for the lead coming off turn four on lap 184 of the 188-lap race, rookie Hendrick driver Brian Vickers and Casey Mears collided, sending Vickers sliding and bringing out the 11th caution flag of the race.

Under NASCAR's rule change from last fall, freezing the field when the yellow comes out rather than letting the competitors race to the flagstand, Gordon got his first Nextel Cup victory of the season, third on Talladega's 2.66-mile oval and the 65th of his NASCAR career.

At first, Earnhardt was posted in front, but replays appeared to show Gordon's No. 24 Chevrolet was about three-quarters of a car length ahead of Earnhardt's No. 8 Monte Carlo when the caution waved. The partisan crowd booed lustily and beer cans and food rained onto the track as Gordon was put back on top and drove slowly to the finish behind the pace truck and in front of Earnhardt.

"The kind of breaks we've been having lately, I wasn't going to get too excited until I crossed the finish line," he said. "I thought they might get the race restarted and I still might have some work to do.

"Beating the DEI cars is difficult to do," Gordon said, referring to both Earnhardt and Michael Waltrip who, between them, had won five straight Cup races at Talladega, including four by Junior.

Gordon said he didn't know if he was ahead of Earnhardt when the caution came out.

"I know I was ahead of him coming out of (turn) three, but we'll let NASCAR make that decision," he said.

Gordon, a four-time Cup champion, led four times for a total of 15 laps.

Earnhardt, who led 11 times for a race-high 57 laps, politely disagreed with NASCAR's decision.

"There at the end, we rolled out to the outside and I got a shove from 48 coming down the back straightaway," Earnhardt said, referring to fourth-place finisher Jimmie Johnson, another of Gordon's teammates.

"I thought I was out ahead of Jeff when the caution came out, but that's not the way NASCAR saw it and I still haven't seen NASCAR's evidence to show me I was not ahead of him when the caution came out. I was a car-length ahead of him when I went past a caution light which was not on.

"We'll just see what they got to show us and we'll go with that. We aren't going to argue and stomp our feet about it. NASCAR makes the rules."

NASCAR spokesman Jim Hunter said a videotape review clearly showed Gordon ahead when the caution lights came on.

"We turned the lights on when the wreck was in progress," Hunter said. "We had a great piece of footage that showed the two cars, so it was really clear-cut that Gordon was in the lead."

Hunter said Tony Eury, Earnhardt's crew chief, looked the video and agreed with NASCAR.

The other part of the controversy was the fact that NASCAR did not get the green flag back out for a race to the finish, keeping it under caution to the end and igniting the fans anger when they realized Gordon was going to win.

"Here and at Daytona we're not going to have a one-lap shootout just because of safety," Hunter said. "We're just not going to do that."

There had already been enough bumping and banging at speeds above 190 mph in a race typical of the recent Cup events at both Talladega and Daytona, the tracks where NASCAR requires horsepower-dampening carburetor restrictor plates to slow the cars.

Cars ran in huge packs, often three- and four-wide throughout and there was passing from front to back on nearly every lap. The lead changed hands 54 times.

Earnhardt and Waltrip had combined to win 10 of the previous 13 races at the two big tracks. But Earnhardt, who is leading the season points, didn't appear too disappointed by finishing second.

"It was a wild race," Earnhardt said. "Everybody was really having a lot of fun out there. Regardless of all the beating and banging, we were all smiles. There was lot of racing and a lot of passing."

With the cars running so close together, and all with about the same horsepower, multicar crashes are nearly inevitable at Talladega and Daytona - and Sunday was no exception.

The "Big One" came on lap 84 when Tony Stewart tapped the rear of Kurt Busch's car near the bottom of the banked track, sending Busch sliding sideways up the banking right in front of a huge pack of cars.

Before the crashing and spinning was through, 10 cars were scattered around the fourth turn. The cars driven by Busch, Derrike Cope and Kenny Wallace had to be hauled off on flatbed trucks. There were no injuries.

Kevin Harvick wound up third, just ahead of Johnson, who was followed by Robby Gordon, Mark Martin, Jeff Burton and Mears.

Waltrip, who won here last fall, ran near the front most of the day but faded at the end to finish 12th.

'NOW I'M THE MAN'
Wednesday, May 12, 2004

Jeff Gordon is older, wiser and definitely back on his game.

"I used to be The Kid," he joked. "Now I'm The Man."

After a couple of relatively quiet seasons - by Gordon's standards - the four-time series champion and his Hendrick Motorsports team are very much the center of attention again.

He's had five straight top-10 finishes, including victories in the last two Nextel Cup events - the 15th time in his career he has won at least two straight.

"It's nice to have momentum," said Gordon, who will go for three in a row Saturday night in Richmond. "A lot of that has to do with the way the team has responded. We've had some bad luck and some bad breaks and they never give up."

The seed for this season's resurgence was planted in 2000, when Gordon and new crew chief Robbie Loomis struggled to a ninth-place finish in the points. It was Gordon's worst since finishing 14th his rookie year.

Although Gordon bounced back with his fourth title the next year, the No. 24 team didn't return to the dominance it once had in the late '90s.

"Well, 2000 was a tough year for us," the 32-year-old driver explained. "We questioned ourselves. Once you overcome adversity, it allows you to overcome it more and more and deal with it in a better way.

"I'm very fortunate that the people at Hendrick Motorsports never lose sight of that. Each week, no matter what's thrown at us, we put it behind us and go to the next week."

Since winning his last title in 2001, Gordon has finished fourth each year while a group of young drivers, including his protégé, Jimmie Johnson, stole the spotlight.

It didn't get any easier for Gordon. Last season, while struggling through a 31-race winless streak, Gordon also had to deal with a highly publicized divorce from his wife of seven years, Brooke. In the end, Gordon and his wife reached a settlement that guaranteed her at least $15.3 million.

Though Gordon and his team appear back on track this season, Loomis is cautious about getting too excited after only 10 races.

"In this sport, it's funny - it doesn't take much to get on a roll and it doesn't take much to go the other way, either," said Loomis, who replaced Ray Evernham, Gordon's crew chief and mentor through his first three championships. "That's why you have to keep evolving as a team.

"A lot of times you need to do things differently, to change as you go along, to keep being successful," Loomis added. "You have to really talk to yourself, to convince yourself not to remain static because then you're not moving forward."

That's where Gordon's experience and attitude come into play.

A crash at Darlington in March relegated Gordon to a 41st-place finish and bumped him to 13th in the points. Since then, he has been on a tear, finishing ninth, third and sixth before the victories at Talladega and California.

"Jeff is the inspiration of this organization," Loomis said. "No matter how bad we are in practice or qualifying or early in a race, he instills confidence in everybody."

Heading into Richmond, Gordon was back up to third in the standings, trailing series leader Dale Earnhardt Jr. by 27 points and Johnson by just two.

One thing that has changed for Gordon and Loomis is the way they are approaching the championship chase in 2004.

NASCAR changed the points system this season, with the top 10 drivers and any others within 400 points of the leader after the first 26 races eligible for the final 10-race "Chase for the Championship."

"I've talked to Will Perdue, who used to play for the Chicago Bulls, and some pro football players and they said their approach was to first make the playoffs, then worry about the championship," Loomis said.

"That's different than the way we've always looked at it, but that's the approach we're taking now. We're going week by week and race by race to be right where we need to be to go after the Nextel Cup championship."

FIFTH CHAMPIONSHIP THREAT
Charlotte, North Carolina, Wednesday, July 7, 2004

In any other season, Jeff Gordon would be a long shot to win the championship.

But under NASCAR's new points system, Gordon is a legitimate threat. After back-to-back victories the past two weeks, he might even be the top contender.

Coming off dominating wins on two very different racetracks - the windy road course at Sonoma and the superspeedway at Daytona - Gordon headed into Sunday's race in Chicago in third place in the standings, 232 points behind leader Jimmie Johnson.

Making up that kind of ground would have been a struggle under the old points system. But this year, NASCAR will reset the field with ten races to go and all drivers in the top 10 will run for the championship.

"If you're leading, you hate this system. And if you're way back, you love it," Gordon said. "It's going to be extremely interesting as to how it all turns out over the final 10 because at that point, basically everything you did all year long is a wash.

"You'd just better hope that your momentum and the experiences you've had are the payoff and you have that in those last 10."

Johnson, Gordon's teammate at Hendrick Motorsports, has not wavered in his dislike for the new points system.

And why should he? He'll have worked hard for 26 races to put himself in position to win his first NASCAR championship. Then, just when it's within his reach, he'll have Gordon bearing down on him in pursuit of his fifth title.

It could be a strain on the four-year-old relationship that began when Gordon became Johnson's mentor, friend and co-owner of Johnson's car.

"It will be different for us," Johnson said. "Obviously, we have raced against each other for wins and competed at that level, but a championship will be a whole new thing."

Because the field will be reset, it's possible any of the drivers eligible for the final 10-race shootout could win the title. But garage insiders already have an idea on how it might play out.

"I think the two Hendrick cars have a really good chance of finishing 1-2 in the championship," said car owner Ray Evernham, who won three championships as Gordon's crew chief. "Jimmie and Jeff both look like they can make a run at it."

Until recently, Gordon was just trying to keep up with Johnson.

Although he has a series-high four victories and won back-to-back races in April at Talladega and California Speedway, the No. 24 team faltered with horrible runs in Charlotte and Dover.

The Charlotte race was the low point of the season. Gordon started third, but the car was never good and they finished 30th, seven laps down from race-winner Johnson.

"Charlotte lit a fire under us," he said. "We had a miserable day and embarrassed ourselves and Rick Hendrick and our sponsors. We've been on a mission ever since."

The rebound began in mid-June at Michigan, when Gordon won the pole and led 81 of the first 88 laps until his engine blew. Despite his 38th-place finish, Gordon showed he was back.

He's won two races since then, starting from the pole each time for three consecutive front-row spots.

"I tell you what, it makes me feel pretty darn good right now, that's for sure," Gordon said. "What a way to get momentum - to be strong week-in and week-out, on totally different types of tracks."

Now he heads to Chicago, one of just four tracks on the circuit where Gordon has yet to win. Despite his failure to reach Victory

Lane there, Gordon has two top-fives and an average finish of 7.6 in three starts at the 1.5-mile speedway.

Gordon, who needs just one more win to tie Cale Yarborough for third on Nextel Cup's modern-era list with 69 victories, would love for it to come at Chicago.

"It would be nice to win at a track that we haven't won on yet," he said. "It's a cool statistic, but that's not my goal.

"My goal is to get better everywhere we go, try to win every race and, ultimately, win the championship. Winning at a track we've never won on would be icing on the cake."

SIGNS OF OLD DOMINANCE
Wednesday, August 11, 2004

As Jeff Gordon crossed the finish line the Brickyard 400, team owner Rick Hendrick yelled into the radio: "Have I told you lately that you are the man?"

The four-time NASCAR champion hasn't heard that much the last two years as he struggled through a pair of mediocre - for him - three-win, fourth-place seasons.

Last year, he went through a frustrating 31-race winless streak, the longest since his first two years (1993-94) in NASCAR's premier stock car series.

Gordon has acknowledged that a messy, expensive and very public divorce from Brooke, his wife of seven years, was part of the problem.

There was also a perception that the well-spoken driver with the movie-star looks appeared to be concentrating more on his next career move than getting his No. 24 Chevrolet team back on track. He has hosted "Saturday Night Live" and appeared on a number of other television shows during that time.

And there was the added distraction of putting together and developing the team he co-owns with Hendrick that fields cars for third-year NASCAR star Jimmie Johnson. Johnson has outshone his boss and teammate with finishes of fifth and second in the points the last two years.

"You know, people don't realize just how competitive Nextel Cup racing is," Gordon said. "When you don't win, they find all kinds of reasons for it. But we just had some rebuilding to do with our team - the cars, the motors and the people."

Whatever the reason, it appears now that NASCAR's "Golden Boy," the driver who won 33 races and two of his championships in a three-year span from 1996 to 1998, is back, better than ever.

Veteran driver and owner Richard Petty, left, and Jeff Gordon share a laugh prior to the start of the NASCAR Winston Cup Ford 400 at Homestead-Miami Speedway, November 17, 2002. (AP Photo/Chuck Burton)

His 69th career victory moved him within seven of Dale Earnhardt, whom Gordon replaced as the biggest star in the sport after Earnhardt was killed in the 2001 Daytona 500.

Gordon's milestone Brickyard win, matching the four Indianapolis open-wheel victories by his early heroes, A.J Foyt, Al Unser and Rick Mears, was just the latest in a series of strong performances.

Over the last eight races, Gordon has driven to three of his five series-leading wins and has finished lower than fifth only once. That streak has moved him within 97 points of Johnson, who is leading the standings.

Gordon hasn't led the points this season. But he has found momentum at just the right time in a year in which NASCAR has changed the way the championship is determined.

Sunday's road race at Watkins Glen is one of only five more events until the new, 10-race "Chase for the Cup" begins. At that point, the top 10 drivers in the standings will start with a separation of only 45 points and race for the title.

A fifth title would move Gordon within two of the record seven, held jointly by Earnhardt and legendary stock car king Richard Petty, whose final race was Gordon's first.

And, at 33, Gordon could just be reaching the prime of his career.

Nobody is likely to match Petty's 200 career victories or Earnhardt's incredible popularity, but the argument is already raging over which of the three is the best ever in the stock car sport.

The latest win at Indianapolis certainly has given Gordon's backers a little more evidence for their case.

Longtime NASCAR star Dale Jarrett, who finished second to Gordon at Indy, was asked where Gordon stands in the pantheon of stars who have raced at the historic track.

"He's probably as good a driver as ever been here," Jarrett said. "He's beat the very best here because everybody brings their best stuff.

"Aside from Daytona, we prepare for this race as much as any that we do. And for that guy to come here and win a little over a third of them is pretty incredible. It shows they have a great team, but they have a great driver right there, too. You have to consider him one of the best drivers of any kind that's ever been here."

Gordon won't get into the debate about who is best at Indy or in NASCAR.

"I don't think anybody will ever know who the best is because I just don't think there's any really fair way to figure that out," Gordon said.

"I try not to put myself in that category because all I care about is winning races and being behind the wheel of a race car. ... That's what really matters to me."

HENDRICK PLANE CRASHES
Martinsville, Virginia, Monday, October 25, 2004

A plane owned by the Hendrick Motorsports organization crashed Sunday on its way to a NASCAR race, killing all 10 people aboard, including the son, brother and two nieces of the owner of one of auto racing's most successful teams.

The Beech 200 took off from Concord, North Carolina, and crashed in the Bull Mountain area about seven miles west of Martinsville's Blue Ridge Regional Airport about 12:30 p.m., said Arlene Murray, spokeswoman for the Federal Aviation Administration.

A spokesman for a funeral home where the bodies were being taken said the dead included the four relatives of Rick Hendrick, owner of Hendrick Motorsports.

The weather in the area was overcast at the time of the crash, according to Jan Jackson of the National Weather Service in Blacksburg.

It was "extremely foggy" in the area of the crash, said Dale Greeson, who lives about a mile from where the plane went down. He said he heard what sounded like a small plane circling overhead around the time of the crash, but did not hear the crash itself.

NTSB spokesman Keith Holloway said investigators were on their way to the crash site, which was in rough terrain, but could not begin their examination until Monday.

Hendrick owns the teams of Jeff Gordon, Jimmie Johnson, Terry Labonte and Brian Vickers, who competed in Sunday's Subway 500 in the Nextel Cup Series at Martinsville Speedway.

NASCAR learned of the plane's disappearance during the race but withheld the information from the Hendrick drivers until afterward, NASCAR spokesman Jim Hunter said. All the Hendrick drivers were summoned to the NASCAR hauler immediately after the race and Johnson, who won the race, was excused from Victory Lane.

"I just feel so bad it's unreal," driver Mark Martin told the Speed Channel after the race. Martin's father, stepmother and half-sister died in 1998 when a private plane his father was piloting crashed in Nevada.

Fog shrouds Bull Mountain and the press area at the staging area for search and rescue for the Hendrick Motorsport plane crash site in Patrick Springs, Virginia. A plane carrying Ricky Hendrick, Rick Hendrick's son and a retired NASCAR driver; John Hendrick, Rick Hendrick's brother and president of the organization; Kimberly and Jennifer Hendrick, John Hendrick's twin daughters; Joe Jackson; Jeff Turner; Randy Dorton, the team's chief engine builder; Scott Latham, a pilot for NASCAR driver Tony Stewart; and pilots Dick Tracy and Liz Morrison crashed on Bull Mountain just west of the Patrick county airport, October 24, 2004. (AP Photo/Steve Helber)

Driver Rusty Wallace, who like Martin is also a pilot, told reporters after the race: "Talladega and this place are the two most dangerous approaches on the circuit. I feel bad that this happened, maybe the states will fix something. ... We all feel like we have professional aviation groups, but obviously something went majorly wrong."

Hendrick Motorsports issued a statement late Sunday asking "that those affected be kept in your thoughts and prayers, and respectfully requests that privacy be considered throughout this difficult time."

Hendrick had been on a season-long celebration of its 20th anniversary in NASCAR's top series. The organization has won five of the series' top titles, three truck series titles, and one Busch series crown.

The team has over 100 Cup series wins, making Hendrick just the second team owner in NASCAR's modern era to surpass that mark.

Hendrick late Sunday identified the dead as: Ricky Hendrick, Rick Hendrick's son and a retired NASCAR driver; John Hendrick, Rick Hendrick's brother and president of the organization; Kimberly and Jennifer Hendrick, John Hendrick's 22-year-old twin daughters; Joe Jackson, an executive with DuPont, sponsor of Gordon's car; Jeff Turner, general manager of Hendrick Motorsports; Randy Dorton, the team's chief engine builder; Scott Lathram, a pilot for NASCAR driver Tony Stewart; and pilots Dick Tracy and Liz Morrison.

Rick Hendrick had recently begun grooming Ricky Hendrick, 24, for a larger role with the company.

Ricky began his career driving a Busch car for his father, but retired in 2002 because of a shoulder injury suffered in a racing accident. His father then made him the owner of the Busch car Vickers drove to the series championship last season, and that Kyle Busch currently pilots.

Hendrick employs 460 workers at the Charlotte, N.C.-based Motorsports compound, which includes race shops and a 15,000-square-foot museum and team store.

The main sign outside the facility was covered with a gray tarp, and the gates were barricaded by deputies who allowed only employees through.

Some of the operation's employees gathered in small groups in the parking lot before going inside the building for about 90 minutes.

Several bouquets of flowers were placed on shrubs below a sign denoting "Papa Joe Hendrick Boulevard," which leads into the compound. Joe Hendrick Jr., who was Rick and John Hendrick's father and also was involved in the company, died in July.

"It's just very tough," said Donnie Floyd, who works on the team of Hendrick driver Terry Labonte. "We are like one big family."

Joe McGovern, a self-described racing fan from nearby Concord who said he knows the family, drove by to pay his respects.

"It's just devastating," he said. "This was just a great racing team and they are also such nice people."

WITH HEAVY HEARTS IT'S BACK TO WORK
Hampton, Georgia, Saturday, October 30, 2004

Jeff Gordon tugged at the thin blue wristband, which contained the message: "Life Is A Team Sport."

Never did those words seem more poignant.

Gordon and the other drivers from Hendrick Motorsports went very public with their grieving on Friday, appearing together at Atlanta Motor Speedway just five days after the plane crash that killed 10 people and devastated their close-knit team.

The son, brother and twin nieces of owner Rick Hendrick were flying to the race in Martinsville when the plane slammed into a mountain not far from the track. The team also lost its general manager and chief engine builder.

"I think they would be proud of us to be able to come out here and just keep doing what we love to do, what they loved being part of," Gordon said. "There will be a time when we can all move on from this tragedy."

Certainly, it won't be this weekend. But, in a sport that carries the somber threat of death at every turn, Gordon and his teammates - Jimmie Johnson, Terry Labonte and Brian Vickers - knew it was time to get back to work.

They practiced in the afternoon. They qualified for Sunday's Nextel Cup race in the evening. They amazed those around them with their vulnerability, but also with their determination to make some sense of it all.

Elliott Sadler was back in his camper, watching on television as the Hendrick drivers and crew chiefs remembered their friends.

"One of the most difficult things I've ever had to sit and watch," Sadler said. "My whole insides were pretty much torn up and just bawling at each emotion they were showing. I felt like I was sharing it with them."

Gordon's wristband is a symbol of the bone-marrow donor organization started by Hendrick after he was diagnosed with leukemia. Now, it takes on a whole new meaning.

"Take time to think about those people you love, how you appreciate them, and thank them while you can," said Robbie Loomis, Gordon's crew chief. "When we're young, we think life goes on forever."

It does go on for those left behind.

Gordon and Johnson are still in contention for the season championship with only four races left. The Atlanta race will likely have a huge impact on their title hopes.

"I've never been so inspired and driven in my life," Gordon said, his somber look turning resolute.

He's second in the standings, trailing Kurt Busch by 96 points. It's an imposing deficit to overcome, but hardly unattainable.

"I think it would be a great story to win this championship," Loomis said. "The biggest thing that's going to help is the support for one another, the love we can give to one another every day, and just doing our job."

Vickers was hit especially hard by the tragedy.

His No. 25 car was owned by Hendrick's 24-year-old son, Ricky, who gave up his own racing career after being injured in a crash. In just two years behind the wall, the younger Hendrick showed plenty of business savvy. In all likelihood, he would have been running the family's entire operation someday.

Vickers came along with his teammates to the infield media center, but he didn't want to answer any questions. He made a short statement, then spent most of the time staring at the floor.

"I lost a dear friend," Vickers said, his voice wavering. "They will all be deeply missed for a long time to come - until we all get a chance to see them again."

Beyond the enormous personal toll, the crash took many of the key players in one of NASCAR's most prominent teams.

Randy Dorton ran the engine-building department, ensuring there was enough power under the hood for Gordon to win all four of his Cup titles and Labonte to capture the second championship of his career.

General manager Jeff Turner ran the business side of things, overseeing a massive operation that employs more than 400 workers at its Charlotte, N.C.-based compound.

Jeff Andrews, who was Dorton's right-hand man, will move up to run the engine department. He already was handling many of the day-to-day duties.

"Randy's organization is extraordinarily deep," said Patrick Perkins, the team's director of marketing. "Randy was the visionary, but those guys below him took care of fulfilling the vision and setting the vision, too."

Rick Hendrick won't be attending Sunday's race, and no one knows when he'll resume his role in the daily operations. In the meantime, he's appointed close confidant Bobby Rice to keep an eye on things.

Rice, partner in a North Carolina accounting firm, has long been involved with Hendrick's massive network of car dealerships. Those who already worked under Turner will take on added responsibilities.

"We will miss the leadership of a person like Jeff Turner," Perkins said. "But he brought us up well. We'll pick up the slack."

FINAL WEEK OF THE CHASE
Charlotte, North Carolina, Wednesday, November 17, 2004

Forget the math or the infinite number of potential scenarios to determine who will win NASCAR's Nextel Cup title.

There should be only one strategy for the five drivers still eligible to win the title Sunday at Homestead-Miami Speedway: win the race and don't worry about what the other competitors are doing.

With five racers separated by 82 points headed into the final event of NASCAR's 10-race Chase for the Nextel Cup Championship, a crew chief could go mad trying to crunch the numbers to figure out what his driver has to do to win.

So why even bother?

"We'll have a 'Go for broke' attitude," said four-time series champion Jeff Gordon. "We have nothing to lose, we'll give it everything we've got, and hope to come out on top.

"We have to win."

Kurt Busch heads into the finale with an 18-point lead over Jimmie Johnson. Gordon trails Busch by 21 points, Dale Earnhardt Jr. is 72 out and Mark Martin is 82 points behind.

The race is so tight that even if Gordon wins and leads the most laps, he can still lose the title if Busch simply finishes second.

The only sure bet is Busch. If he wins the race, he wins his first series title no matter what the others do.

Under the current scoring system, a win earns 180 points, a last-place finish gets 34 points and all the positions in between are staggered. Five-point bonuses are given to any driver who leads a lap, and an additional five-point bonus is awarded for leading the most laps in a race.

So if Busch wins the race, he is guaranteed 185 points. Even if Johnson, or Gordon, or anyone else finishes second and earned two bonuses - five points for leading one lap, and five more for leading the most laps - it would still only equal 180 points, not enough to overcome the lead Busch already has.

"I think if I'm Kurt, I would be really nervous," said Earnhardt. "He's in the situation where, you know, it's really basically up to him and his team to win or lose it."

Earnhardt and Martin have a much tougher battle ahead because, for all practical purposes, it's a three-man chase. Both of them can only hope to play the spoiler.

At 72 points back, Earnhardt needs a terrific finish and hope the three drivers ahead of him all have horrible finishes.

If Junior won the race and led the most laps, Busch would have to finish 29th or worse and not lead a lap for Earnhardt to win the title. But Earnhardt would still have to contend with Gordon and Johnson and hope both of them also finished well behind him.

"We dug ourselves a pretty big hole, and it will be difficult to climb out and still win this championship," Earnhardt said. "We're going to have to be the best team at Homestead as well as the luckiest.

"'I think the Boston Red Sox kind of showed everybody this year what a team can achieve by not giving up, so we'll go into Homestead as a team still with a chance to win the championship."

Martin is in the same situation. Still searching for his first series title, he's stopped thinking about how to win it and focused instead on the only thing he can control.

"We are 82 out, but we still have a shot, but it really doesn't matter because we are going there to try and win the (race) and that's really all we can do," Martin said.

The points scenario is similar to the 1992 race, when four drivers battled for that title.

In the season-ending event at Atlanta Motor Speedway, the late Davey Allison started with a 30-point lead over the late Alan Kulwicki. Allison was 40 points up on Bill Elliott.

Allison needed to finish sixth or better to clinch the title, but after running sixth for much of the race, he crashed with Ernie Irvan. Kulwicki and Elliott were left to decide the title, and because Kulwicki led the most laps in the race, he clinched the 10-point bonus.

Elliott won the race, Kulwicki finished second and won the title because he led a single lap more than Elliott.

It could get just as wild at Homestead.

GORDON AND JOHNSON FALL SHORT
Homestead, Florida, Monday, November 22, 2004

Rick Hendrick's pain would not have been completely soothed by joining Jimmie Johnson or Jeff Gordon to celebrate a Nextel Cup championship.

Still, the drivers desperately wanted to deliver NASCAR's biggest prize to their owner.

Johnson and Gordon each led the Nextel Cup points race at various times during Sunday's season-ending Ford 400, but neither could finish the job and bring Hendrick Motorsports what would have been its sixth NASCAR title in 20 years. Johnson finished in second place, eight points behind champion Kurt Busch.

"The one thing Jeff and I can both look back and say at our teams - and Rick in his heart feels this way, too - if we did everything we could possibly do," Johnson said. "When you go to bed at night knowing that, you sleep a lot easier."

Hendrick was at the race, watching his teams for the first time since an October 24 plane crash near Martinsville, Virginai, killed 10, including his son, his brother, two nieces and employees. Both Johnson and Gordon said his presence added significance to what already was destined to be the year's most important race.

"It's a disappointment, no matter what," said Gordon, who ended the year third, 16 points shy of becoming the third NASCAR driver to win five series titles. "But knowing we had an opportunity to do something really special like that made it that much more meaningful - so it also makes it that much more disappointing."

The revamped NASCAR scoring system - a 10-race chase to the finish among the top 10 drivers - was designed with the hopes of adding extra intrigue to the season's final races, and its inaugural run delivered. Five drivers came to Homestead with a chance to claim the Nextel Cup title, four seeking their first championship.

Johnson was the hottest driver coming in, with four victories in his last five starts. He needed another Sunday, and fell just short.

"For the loss of so many people that were there, it's amazing that we were able to finish where we did and have the comeback that we did," Johnson said. "I wish we could have gotten the job done, but we can go to bed tonight knowing that we gave 100 percent, that we gave everything we could."

Dale Earnhardt Jr. and Mark Martin both realistically needed to win the race and hope that Busch, Johnson and Gordon all finished well back. That didn't happen.

Johnson finished second, Gordon third and Busch fifth - resulting in the tightest championship race in NASCAR history. Martin was 11th Sunday and fourth in final points; Earnhardt was 23rd in the last race, fifth for the year.

"The car was really good at one point, but from there on out it was the worst car I ever drove," Earnhardt said.

With 75 laps to go, Busch, Gordon and Johnson were separated in the title chase by only two points - and Martin loomed just 23 points behind Busch. Martin fell to 26th place when he pitted for a flat tire on lap 229, a problem that sent him 96 points behind the three chase leaders and ended his chances.

"With the way things turned out, the best we could have done was fourth, and we did that," Martin said.

Johnson led the series with eight wins this year, but will spend the next few months wondering how to get eight points better.

"If it's meant to be, it's meant to be," Johnson said. "And it wasn't in the cards for us this year."

The race went down to the wire, just as NASCAR hoped. A green-white-checkered restart at the end capped the season, with Gordon starting the single-file final chase in third, Johnson fourth and Busch fifth.

There wasn't much either of the challengers could do at that point, and Busch hung on for the title.

"It wasn't our day, boys," Gordon said over his team radio moments after the race ended. "It wasn't our year. But we made a hell of an effort. Now we'll go back and try to get them next year."

FANS 'SALUTE' GORDON AT TALLADEGA
Talladega, Alabama, Monday, April 30, 2007

At the track where Dale Earnhardt dominated, and on the day he would have turned 56, Jeff Gordon scored career victory No. 77. It was the fitting venue, the perfect day, for Gordon to move past Earnhardt on NASCAR's wins list. And, as expected, it was wildly unpopular.

Fans littered the track with debris Sunday as Gordon crossed the finish line under caution at Talladega Superspeedway to move into sixth place on the win list.

"I never caused a riot before for winning well, maybe once or twice," Gordon laughed.

It was the same reaction he received last week in Phoenix when he tied Earnhardt's mark and flew a No. 3 flag on his victory lap. That gesture didn't sit well with Earnhardt fans, even though Dale Earnhardt Jr. called the tribute classy and urged his "Red Army" of supporters to stop throwing beer cans out of safety concerns.

"I thought Junior had more power," Gordon said. "I thought they'd throw toilet paper, which is what he asked them to throw. I saw maybe one roll."

But Talladega is Earnhardt country. The Intimidator won 10 times here, and his legion of fans adopted his son following Earnhardt's 2001 death. The fans turn the grandstands into a sea of red, and when Junior charges to the front the roar is deafening.

It's what made this the perfect place for Gordon to surpass the seven-time champion. Although their fans mix like oil and water, Earnhardt and Gordon were pals. They shared a competitive rivalry on the track and a healthy friendship away from it.

Earnhardt would have been proud, and Gordon was conflicted about it.

"On one side I just want to jump up and down and be fired up about getting 77 here at Talladega where three-quarters of the grandstands were pulling against us," Gordon said. "And then on the other side, I respected Dale so much, learned so much from him, today being his birthday and knowing how many of those people up there wanted to see Dale Earnhardt Jr. win today it's tough.

"I certainly didn't want to start a riot, and hopefully nobody got injured. But I wanted to break that record. I keep going back and forth. Why did it have to happen at Talladega?"

The ending was anticlimactic and confusing, finishing under caution with Gordon unsure if he'd actually won. Nobody was quite sure after two separate accidents on the first lap of a two-lap shootout to the finish froze the field and had NASCAR scrambling to make sense of the finish.

Gordon, who started from the pole, ran up front early but was 14th on a restart with 10 laps to go. He stormed to the front, and with three laps to go passed Jamie McMurray for the lead a split-second before a caution came out.

It set up a the green-white-checkered flag finish, with Gordon out front on the restart. But before the field reached full speed, a wreck far behind the leaders brought out the caution and effectively ended the race.

NASCAR makes only one attempt to complete the race in over-time, and if a caution comes out, the field is instantly frozen. So when Elliott Sadler bumped the back of Greg Biffle to trigger a wreck, Gordon was essentially the winner.

But it was unclear as the action continued.

Tony Stewart, embroiled in controversy all week for likening NASCAR to pro wrestling, was knocked into the wall far ahead of the first accident. He bounced off the outside wall, slid down the track and into the inside wall, then stood fuming on the apron as he waited for the field to pass. He made an angry gesture at McMurray and David Gilliland as they passed under caution.

With all that going on, Gordon was too hesitant to claim the win.

As the field slowly headed to the flag, and the beer cans began to fly over the fence and onto his car, he accepted it.

"I love it," he radioed. "That's awesome."

Gordon made one attempt at a celebratory burnout, which he later admitted was a bad decision because it egged fans on to throw more debris at him.

Track officials warned fans they would be arrested for throwing anything on the track, and 10 fans were detained as Gordon's crew frantically called for security help to get the team spotter out of the stands.

"It don't look like it's something you can control," Earnhardt Jr. sighed.

NASCAR condemned the debris throwing.

"It's very unfortunate a few unruly fans can ruin things for a lot of people," spokesman Jim Hunter said. "The track put a lot of effort into preventing this type of behavior. Our fans are passionate, but this type of behavior doesn't represent a majority of our fans."

Earnhardt Jr., who made a brief run at the victory, finished seventh. But unlike last week, when he visited Gordon in Victory Lane, he stayed away from the celebration.

"I told him this week, I said, `You win this one and I ain't coming into Victory Lane this time. That caused too much trouble,'" Junior said. "He's a great race car driver. I knew years ago he would eventually pass my old man. I think he has the opportunity to pass a couple more."

Jimmie Johnson, Gordon's teammate, finished second as Hendrick Motorsports cars continued their season-long domination. Hendrick drivers have won six of the first nine races.

Kurt Busch was third, Gilliland fourth and McMurray finished fifth. Kevin Harvick was sixth, followed by Earnhardt, David Stremme, Ryan Newman and Martin Truex Jr.

Stewart, who had a disastrous race but was still in position to race for the win at the end, wound up 28th.

Ironically, he needed a debris caution something he questioned the integrity of this week to save his race. The two-time champion was penalized for speeding on pit road early in the race and went one lap down after returning to the pits.

But he got the lap back shortly after when NASCAR found debris on the track and called for a caution. He struggled on the restart, though, and fell out of the draft. But he got another break moments later when Clint Bowyer wrecked.

GORDON MORE LIKE ERNHARDT THAN FANS ADMIT
Talladega, Alabama, Monday, April 30, 2007

Accept it, race fans: Dale Earnhardt and Jeff Gordon were buddies.

The old man respected the kid and took time to help him adjust to NASCAR's politics. Earnhardt recognized Gordon as a huge talent and cherished their on-track battles, knowing each victory was a win over a driver destined to go down as one of the best.

It's fact, yet many Earnhardt fans choose to ignore it.

They pretend the two drivers were bitter rivals, two very different men with nothing in common. No matter how hard he tries or what he accomplishes, Earnhardt fans are adamant that Gordon simply does not stack up against The Intimidator.

Turns out, though, that Gordon is a whole lot more like Earnhardt than anyone imagined.

Gordon proved it Sunday with career victory No. 77, which pushed him past Earnhardt for sixth place on NASCAR's list. It came at Talladega Superspeedway, where the crowd is virtually all pro-Earnhardt, and on the day Earnhardt would have celebrated his 56th birthday.

The feat was met with a shower of beer cans thrown from the stands.

The record book will show that Gordon took the lead with three laps to go and then won under caution during over-time. But the victory seemed destined hours earlier when he made an Earnhardtesque stand in the prerace drivers' meeting.

NASCAR warned the drivers that there's a fine line between skillfully bump-drafting and aggressive driving. Gordon respectfully disagreed. In a room packed with his peers, he spoke with NASCAR president Mike Helton about the dangers the drivers were about to face.

"I absolutely don't think there is a fine line," he began. "We're not able to mandate it ourselves. You guys have to mandate it because we've got the adrenaline flowing. We're competitors out there trying to win. And we see one guy push another guy, it allows us each to continue to do it more and more and more.

"And, yeah, obviously, you can't do it in the corners, but we still do it. Even on the straightaways, it's about judging the speed, and we're still wrecking on the straightaways. I don't think that should be happening at all. We can make a great, exciting race out there. And no offense to your warning, but when you drop the green, I guarantee we're going to be doing it."

And that, Tony Stewart, is how to make a point.

Days after Stewart exposed the sport to ridicule by comparing it to professional wrestling on his national radio show, Gordon calmly made a point to NASCAR that benefited all 43 drivers in the field.

For a guy who has resisted replacing the voice that was lost when Earnhardt died in 2001, Gordon certainly appeared a perfect fit for the role Sunday.

He insisted after his victory that too much was being made of his stand even though the race was much tamer by Talladega standards and might have been because of his comments.

"It was kind of a spur of the moment thing," he said. "I wanted to go see (NASCAR) before the drivers' meeting, and I didn't get a chance to, and something sparked inside of me and I just had to say something. I don't know if that made a difference or not, but (the race) was one of the best.

"But it had nothing to do with trying to set an example for others of how you go about it. I always try to go about saying things to NASCAR as gingerly as I can to try to get my point across, but not put anything down or take away from anything or anybody."

Former series champion Kurt Busch said Gordon has "always been the lead guy to be politically correct with NASCAR."

"Gordon is very selective with his words," he said.

Teammate Jimmie Johnson said the prerace comments were something most drivers would not have been comfortable making.

"If many other drivers would have spoken up and said what Jeff did in the drivers' meeting, it would have come off wrong and people would have laughed," Johnson said. "It wouldn't have come off the same way. But Jeff is at that spot in his career and he's so well spoken and comes from a fair place when he's speaking about those things, that people are listening."

The garage has lacked that presence since Earnhardt's fatal accident. Gordon insists he doesn't want to fill that void, and Stewart proved last week that while his message may be valid, his delivery lacks the finesse Earnhardt perfected.

"I know that Jeff doesn't want to be Dale," Johnson said. "He wants to be himself and do things his own way. I know he doesn't want to be in this position to be the voice of the drivers, but he almost has this responsibility that's developing for him whether he wants it or not."

WILLING TO TAKE RISKS FOR MORE WINS
Talladega, Alabama, Wednesday, August 1, 2007

Jeff Gordon longs for the good old days.

The four-time NASCAR champion doesn't think his best days are behind him, just that he would practically be a lock for another title if it weren't for the Chase for the Nextel Cup championship.

Before the Chase was instituted in 2004, every race on the schedule counted toward the championship and Gordon's 371-point lead over Denny Hamlin heading into Sunday's race at Pocono the 21st of 36 races would mean only a collapse of major proportions could have derailed another championship bid.

Instead, under the Chase format, the first 26 races are considered the regular season and the final 10 make up the championship battle for the top 12 drivers. Once they get past Richmond on September 8, the points for each of the dozen contenders will be evened at 5,000, with an additional 10-point bonus for each regular-season win the only edge available.

But Gordon, who has four wins this season, isn't worried even though he knows it's tougher to win a title now.

"Even though you'd rather the championship, in my opinion, be all the races, I understand what it takes in those last 10 to be good," said Gordon, whose last title came in 2001. "You've got to have good fortune going your way and you have to have fast race cars.

"We've been doing that consistently, so I still feel really good about the championship."

He has been amazingly consistent so far this season.

Coming off a solid third-place finish last Sunday at Indianapolis, Gordon, who will turn 36 on Saturday, has 13 top-fives and 18 top-10s in 20 starts.

The only time he has finished outside the top 10 since a 12th-place run at Atlanta in March and the only time he has failed to finish a race this season was in May at Charlotte, where he crashed out of the Coca-Cola 600 and finished 41st.

Not even losing suspended crew chief Steve Letarte for six races because of a technical violation in June at Sonoma has slowed Gordon down.

In the four races so far without Letarte, Gordon has finished second, fifth, ninth and third.

"I'm excited because we've got a very strong, consistent team and we don't have a crew chief right now," Gordon said. "I think when Steve comes back, it's only going to heighten us and make us stronger for what we've had to go through without him."

If Gordon has any concern at all it's that all four of his wins this season came during a seven-week stretch that began at Phoenix in April and ended at Pocono in June. That means he has gone six races without visiting Victory Lane.

With just six races until the start of the Chase, Gordon said his team is mostly focused on getting more wins to get a step up on competition for the start of the postseason.

"Bonus points is what it's all about for us," he said. "That means we have to be risky. You know we can afford to lose some points by taking bigger risks and possibly getting those bonus points and wins, and that momentum that we really need."

Also on Gordon's mind is Tony Stewart. The two-time Cup champion has begun one of his traditional second-half hot streaks.

After struggling with all kinds of bad luck through the first half of the season, Stewart suddenly is the winner of two straight races and looking like Gordon's main competition come September.

Even after NASCAR docked Stewart 25 points and fined him $25,000 this week for cursing during a postrace TV interview at Indy, he is fifth in the standings. If the Chase began this week, those two wins would mean Stewart would be just 20 points behind Gordon going into the last 10 races.

"You know they're a strong team," Gordon said. "Because of the Chase, you know, anybody is a threat for the championship, especially if they're showing strong runs and winning races at this point in the season.

"I know we're going to have to beat Tony, among other guys. You know, I still think that we're a little bit more consistent than them, but I think right now they've got a little bit of an edge on us in speed and we've got to find it. We've got to get after that."

GORDON WINS AT TALLADEGA
Talladega, Alabama, Monday, October 8, 2007

It's not in Jeff Gordon's nature to go slow, and asking the four-time series champion to ride aimlessly around in the back of the pack is unheard of.

But with all the unknowns surrounding Sunday's race at Talladega Superspeedway, it seemed to be the safest strategy. Still, he resisted, and even told car owner Rick Hendrick he wouldn't do it.

He apparently had a change of heart, agreeing to turn parade laps for much of the race before surging past Jimmie Johnson on the final lap and holding off his teammate to become the career victory leader at restrictor-plate tracks.

Jeff Gordon leads the pack through the tri-oval on the last lap to win the NASCAR Nextel Cup UAW-Ford 500 auto race at Talladega Superspeedway, October 7, 2007. (AP Photo/Glenn Smith)

"It was the hardest race I've ever had to be in. I've never had that type of mind-set before," Gordon said. "I've never done that before. I even told Rick Hendrick earlier in the week that some guys were talking about that strategy, and I can't do it I think we've got to get out there and race and let the chips fall where they may.

"I changed that ... and it was tough because I don't like just going out there and riding in the back. I want to be out there battling for the lead and leading laps."

He parlayed his decision into his 12th career plate win and fifth victory this season, and moved back on top of the points standings.

He leads Johnson by nine points with six races remaining in the Chase for the championship.

But it was bizarre way to do it by Gordon's standards.

Fears over the Car of Tomorrow's plate debut and former Formula One champion Jacques Villeneuve's first Nextel Cup event had the entire field concerned the race would be one big demolition derby.

So Gordon decided he'd avoid the mess by staying in the back, and found himself yawning in his race car for the first time in his career.

Gordon had a horrible qualifying effort he started 34th and it put him at the back, where he never tried to move from. He then suffered a late-race setback when he pulled out of his pit with a hose hanging from his car, earning a pass-through penalty that seemed to take him out of contention.

Still, he sat back, resisting the urge to charge to the front.

"It was terrible, I am telling you that was the hardest thing I've ever had to do in a race car," Gordon said. "I like to think that I have pretty good patience, but that's beyond patience.

"There's just nothing fun about that, but I knew it was the smart thing."

A master at working the draft, Gordon eventually marched toward the front and had moved into the top 15 as the race neared its completion. With six laps to go, he was in the middle of a Hendrick Motorsports charge that saw Johnson, Gordon and Casey Mears surge to the front of the pack.

Gordon was stuck behind Johnson, though, and waited until the last lap to make a move toward the front. He finally jumped up high, squeezing in between Johnson and the Penske cars of Ryan Newman and Kurt Busch.

Just as Johnson tried to block him, two-time series champion Tony Stewart slid onto Gordon's bumper and gave him a huge push into the lead. Gordon led just one lap the last one to complete a season sweep at Talladega.

"I wasn't happy with getting passed, but that would have been the situation with anybody," said Johnson, who finished second. "To get that close and not win is a letdown. There must have been stuff going on behind me that I couldn't see, but Jeff could in his mirror, and he pulled up and got in front of the 20 (Stewart) and was able to take advantage of that push."

Dave Blaney was third in the best finish this year for a Toyota driver. Title contender Denny Hamlin was fourth and was followed by Ryan Newman, who was leading late in his Dodge, and Mears.

Chase driver Kurt Busch was seventh and Stewart, who was in position to win this race very late, had two strategic moves backfire and was shuffled back to eighth.

This race blew open the Chase for the championship standings, as Gordon and Johnson positioned themselves for a Hendrick battle toward the title. Third-place driver Clint Bowyer finished 11th, but fell 63 points behind the leader.

Stewart dropped 154 points out and everyone else is more than 200 points behind.

The entire industry was tense about this race leading up to the green flag because of a combination of the CoT and Villeneuve, who was widely criticized for picking Talladega for his first start.

But Villeneuve, who qualified sixth, dropped to the very back of the pack at the start and stayed out of everyone's way as he quietly finished 21st.

"I'm glad that I didn't create any problems with the drivers," he said. "The finger was being pointed before the race, and that was understandable. The goal was to stay out of trouble and not make enemies."

The garage-wide fear of multiple wrecks because of dangerous driving conditions everyone expected from the CoT didn't materialize until the first big accident with 44 laps to go. And that was more of a fluke than it was a product of Talladega's treacherous racing Bobby Labonte had some sort of mechanical failure that caused his car to squirt down the track and into Chase driver Kyle Busch.

The contact started an 11-car accident that also collected title contenders Matt Kenseth and Hamlin, although Hamlin suffered only cosmetic damage.

But it destroyed Busch and Kenseth's cars, and marked the second consecutive week that title favorite Busch found himself in the wrong place. He was wrecked last week by Dale Earnhardt Jr., and has gone from 10 points out of the lead two weeks ago to seventh in the standings, 260 points out.

"It's unfortunate for our Chase chances, but we knew that Talladega was going to be our mulligan, we circled it on the calendar that this was going to be the one we were going to wreck in," Busch said. "The team of course wants to be optimistic, and they want me to be optimistic, but I'm sorry, it's the realism that sets in that you are so far back that it's going to take a lot to get back in this deal."

Trouble also hit Chase drivers Jeff Burton and Martin Truex Jr., who both suffered from engine problems that ended their race early. Truex finished 42nd, Burton was 43rd and both declared their title hopes over.

"I suspect this is just too much for us to overcome regarding the championship," Burton said.

Truex concurred.

"Without any freaky luck for anyone else, we're pretty much out of it," he said.

The issues with the engines, built by both Dale Earnhardt Inc. and Richard Childress Racing, put a fear in the other five teams who use the same motors and it came true when Earnhardt's blew up.

Earnhardt, trying to end a 55-race winless streak in his final event at DEI with crew chief Tony Eury Jr., was relegated to a 40th-place finish after leading 31 laps early. Eury is moving to Hendrick Motorsports next week to prepare for Junior's arrival at the end of the season.

"We had a good car, we led some, we got the people on their feet. I thought we could win it," Earnhardt said. "I'm sad for Martin more than anything. We have a gremlin in there."

That "gremlin" had title contenders Bowyer and Kevin Harvick on edge, worrying about the durability of their own motors. Both made it to the finish, but neither had anything to challenge the Hendrick duo.

MARCH CONTINUES TOWARD 5TH NEXTEL CUP TITLE
Concord, North Carolina, Sunday, October 14, 2007

There was a time not too long ago when Jeff Gordon wondered if he'd ever win another race.

His personal life was in shambles, and a long losing streak had the four-time series champion doubting himself for the first time in his storied NASCAR career. The wins were few and far between, and the consistent title contender had turned into a perpetual also-ran.

Now five years later, Gordon can't be stopped he's ticking off wins, marching toward another title and, no coincidence here, has never been happier.

With his sixth win of the season Saturday night at Lowe's Motor Speedway, Gordon opened a healthy 68-point lead in the Nextel Cup points standings. He then celebrated with friends and family, including his only sister, Kimberly Coykendall, who through bad timing had missed the first 80 victories of his Cup career.

As he approaches his first wedding anniversary with wife Ingrid and delights in the joys of fatherhood with infant daughter Ella, Gordon insists he'll be satisfied no matter where he winds up in the final season standings.

"I'm going to tell you right now, I don't care what happens with the championship. This is my year," Gordon said. "Even with the wins that we've had so far, the kind of year on and off the racetrack, for me personally, it's just been the most incredible year."

One that seems destined to end with the fifth championship that has eluded NASCAR's Golden Boy for the past six seasons.

The 22-year-old kid who sobbed in Victory Lane after his first Cup win here back in 1994 matured into one of the most dominant drivers in series history. He reeled off 56 wins and stormed to four championships in a seven-year span from 1995 to 2001.

Along the way, though, his picture-perfect marriage to former NASCAR model Brooke Sealey crumbled. He was 30, at the top of his profession and had more money than he ever dreamed possible. But living in Florida, isolated from family, friends and the NASCAR community, he realized just how miserable he was.

The couple entered into a nasty, public divorce in 2002 that captivated the garage area and coincided with the worst losing streak of his career. The one driver who contended each and every week was in a nearly yearlong slump, failing to visit Victory Lane for an unheard of span of 31 races.

But when he finally broke the streak, using a cold-hearted bump-and-run on Rusty Wallace with three laps to go at Bristol, it hardly kick started his comeback. He knocked down wins every now and again, but wasn't quite a threat for the title and missed the Chase for the championship in 2005.

Team owner Rick Hendrick responded with an immediate crew chief change, promoting one-time parts clerk Steve Letarte into the biggest job of his short career. Letarte came to Hendrick as a 15-year-old enrolled in a work-study program, and spent nine years working his way up to the most pressure-packed job in the company.

They instantly clicked and have been on a high-speed comeback ever since.

"Steve waited a year, could have been a crew chief earlier, to wait for Jeff Gordon, and that chemistry (between them) has been unbelievable," Hendrick said.

Gordon has nine wins in his 77 races with Letarte, and they have been flawless this season while building a lead of more than 300 points during the "regular season." It was all wiped out when the Chase began, but Gordon has quickly taken command of the title hunt.

With five races remaining, it looks to be Gordon's title to lose, and Hendrick believes it's a direct correlation to his personal life.

"I think I see a real happy Jeff Gordon," Hendrick said. "I think that his life outside of racing is probably the best it's ever been, especially with his little girl."

This resurgence has helped Gordon continue his assault on the record books. He passed the late Dale Earnhardt for sixth on the career wins list this spring, and with 81 career victories, he's poised to shoot up the standings.

He needs just three wins to pass Cale Yarborough for fifth, and four victories will slide him past Bobby Allison and Darrell Waltrip. Gordon will never touch Richard Petty's mark of 200 victories, but there's no reason to doubt he can claim No. 2 and pass David Pearson's 105 wins.

Gordon didn't want to speculate when asked Saturday night if he had 25 wins left in his tank.

"A couple years ago, I didn't think I had any left in me," Gordon said. "So right now, we're just having one of those spectacular seasons. We're just going to try to finish it out and see what we get, and next year is a whole new season. Who knows?"

BEST OF FRIENDS BATTLE FOR ULTIMATE PRIZE
Hampton, Georgia, Monday, October 29, 2007

They're teammates. They're boss and employee. They're the best of friends.

Only one can be the champion.

Jimmie Johnson and Jeff Gordon, who look as though they were peeled off the pages of a fashion magazine and drive even better, have turned the Chase for the Nextel Cup championship into their own personal showdown.

Mano-a-mano, with everyone else just along for the ride.

"It's going to be a fight to end," Johnson promised.

Gordon is still leading the Nextel Cup standings, but had his advantage shaved to a mere nine points when Johnson won Sunday's Pep Boys Auto 500 at Atlanta Motor Speedway. With only three races to go, no one else in the Chase is within 100 points.

Despite their close relationship away from the track, there's little doubt that Johnson and Gordon are fierce rivals once they get behind the wheel. This isn't Formula One, where teams often have a strict pecking order for their drivers.

May the best man win this one.

"There's more drama when you have two teammates racing for a championship," Johnson said. "It's not like we are out there just giving each other position and pulling by saying, 'Hi, buddy, go on,' and 'No, sorry, you go through.' It's far from that, and I think that's putting a lot of drama in our sport."

Not for anyone else, though.

This is a two-man party, or some might call it the perfect storm for all those fans who view Gordon and Johnson as a little too polished for a sport with hard-scrabble roots, who see them as two pampered racers who just happen to have the best equipment year in and year out.

"It's easy to criticize from the outside," said Gordon, who finished seventh in Atlanta. "You can't buy a championship in this thing. There are so many guys out there spending a lot of money, hiring the best people and trying to beat us."

All those drivers might as well get started on 2008. Barring a stunning collapse by the Hendrick Motorsports teammates over the next three weeks and what are the chances of that? this season has come down to two possible scenarios: Either Johnson will be hoisting the Cup for the second year in a row, or Gordon will take home his sixth series championship.

On Sunday, Johnson spent most of the day lurking behind the leaders, finally moving to the front just three laps from the end of the scheduled 325-lap event. For that, he could thank crew chief Chad Knaus, who made a brilliant audible in the pits.

Tom Brady would have been proud of this one.

When Knaus spotted leader Kyle Busch have trouble in the pits, he made the call to go with two tires instead of four. Johnson got out of the pits first and pulled in behind Denny Hamlin, who decided to stay out and hope he had enough rubber and gas to remain in the lead.

"When that caution came out, we knew we didn't have a car capable of winning at that point," Knaus said. "Track position was going to be important."

That was apparent right away.

Hamlin's car conked out as prepared to take the green, setting off a demolition derby behind the leader. Afterward, his team found water in the carburetor, an unexplained problem that deceived the crew into thinking there was enough fuel to get to the finish.

Martin Truex, who led a race-high 135 laps, smashed into the back of Hamlin's sputtering machine and finished 31st. Busch, who was out front for 98 laps, spun into the infield grass and was relegated to 17th.

"I hate it for the guys behind us who got caught up in the wreck," Hamlin said. "We felt like it was good or we wouldn't have risked it."

Having another charmed year, Johnson barely slipped by Hamlin to grab the lead. Carl Edwards and Dale Earnhardt Jr. also got through, setting up a two-lap shootout when the green flag came out again on lap 328.

There was no dramatic finish, however. Something snapped in the rear of Earnhardt's car coming out of turn one, sending him into the wall. He collected Jamie McMurray, who had been running fifth, and the race ended under yellow to give Johnson his eighth win of the season and second in a row.

"Today wasn't the best day for our car," said Johnson, who swept both Atlanta races this season. "Circumstances at the end really worked out for us."

Edwards was second, shaking off the stinging criticism he received for a confrontation with teammate Matt Kenseth after the previous week's event at Martinsville.

Edwards was followed across the finish line by hometown favorite Reed Sorenson, Kenseth, Jeff Burton and Clint Bowyer, who
remained third in the 12-man Chase, but still trails Gordon by 111
points, four less than when the race began.

It's hard to imagine Gordon and Johnson having the sort of
trouble that nearly brought the Roush Fenway Racing teammates
to blows.

Gordon is technically listed as the owner of Johnson's car and
served in his wedding party. On race day, their friendship goes on
hiatus for a few hours, but they never lose that respect for each
other.

"Whoever outperforms the other guy is going to be champion,
the way this thing is shaking out," Johnson said. "I know his weaknesses, the weaknesses of his team, and I'm going to do anything I
can to exploit any weakness I can find."

And when the season is done, they'll shake hands no matter
who ends up with the Cup.

"There are some teammates situations out there where there's
not as much love flowing around and guys are not being as good as
they need to be as teammates," Johnson said. "But at Hendrick,
that's something we work really hard on."

It's working just fine.

JOHNSON TAKES COMMAND OF TITLE CHASE
Avondale, Arizona, Monday, November 12, 2007

Nobody could touch Jeff Gordon in his prime, a three-year
stretch when he won 33 races and consecutive championships.

That was almost 10 years ago, and few thought they'd ever see
a driver capable of dominating the way Gordon once did.

Until Jimmie Johnson came along.

Johnson took command of the Nextel Cup championship Sunday, winning at Phoenix International Raceway to open a daunting
lead over his teammate in the race to the title. It was his 10th win of
the season most since Gordon won 13 in 1998 and barring a collapse
in next week's finale, Johnson will become the first driver to win
consecutive championships since Gordon did it in 1997 and 1998.

But Johnson doesn't want to be compared to his mentor, the
four-time series champion.

"I certainly don't want to be called the next Jeff Gordon. I am Jimmie Johnson. I've always done it my way," he said. "If you look at our driving styles, our setups, look at everything we do, we are on opposite ends. We do have some common interests, we are close friends.

"But I am not Jeff Gordon, so let's just get that out of the way."

No, he's not Gordon. But his work on the track makes it impossible not to draw the comparisons.

"They're just unbelievably good," said Matt Kenseth, the 2003 champion. "They're as good as any group I've seen, including Jeff in his heyday when he was winning 10 races a year and the championship by over a hundred points."

Johnson can realistically do the same.

The defending Nextel Cup champion, heads to next week's season finale in Homestead, Florida, with a comfortable 86-point lead over Gordon. He needs to finish just 18th or better to win his second championship in just six seasons.

"It's over. It's over," conceded Gordon. "Even if we win it, it's because they have problems. While we'll accept it, we don't want to do it that way.

"Those guys have flat-out killed everybody. And you've got to give credit where credit is due."

Johnson was subdued in Victory Lane, and refused to claim the title.

"Homestead is going to be a stressful weekend. We've got seven more days, I'm just going to try to keep my mind clear and focus on the things we need to do," Johnson said. "This is kind of where we were last year. We just have to go down there and be smart and see how it shakes out."

Gordon was off all day. He had a tire rub after making contact with Kevin Harvick, and finished a disappointing 10th.

It was a crushing performance on a day when Johnson raced to his fourth consecutive victory. He became the first driver to win four straight in a season since Gordon did in 1998.

Gordon, who hand-picked Johnson to join Hendrick Motorsports when the team expanded to four cars in 2002, marveled at how strong his protégé has been during this championship hunt.

It's put it nearly out of reach for Gordon, who dominated the "regular season" and opened a lead of more than 300 points before the field was reset for the Chase.

"Unless you lead every lap and beat Jimmie Johnson to win the race, we don't have a shot," Gordon said. "We're just coming up short at a crucial time. Those guys have just knocked it out of the ballpark, and it would be tough to beat that even if we were hitting on all eight cylinders."

Although it will take a total collapse next week by a team that rarely falters for Johnson to not win the championship, crew chief Chad Knaus wasn't ready to claim the Cup just yet.

"Obviously were real happy to extend the points lead," Knaus said. "But going into Homestead, you never know. You never know what's going to happen.

"We could easily have an issue and not finish the race. We just have to stay focused and keep our heads down."

Greg Biffle finished second and Matt Kenseth, his Roush Fenway Racing teammate, was third. Tony Stewart was fourth and was followed by Ryan Newman, Harvick, and Martin Truex Jr.

Kyle Busch, who was trying to become the first driver to win three of NASCAR's national races at the same track on the same weekend, finished eighth. Busch won the Truck Series race here on Friday, the Busch Series race on Saturday, but never made it all the way to the front in the Cup event after starting 38th.

The race mathematically eliminated everyone but Johnson and Gordon from title contention, so regardless of what happens in Homestead, Hendrick Motorsports will win its seventh Cup title.

But it was Johnson and his No. 48 team that have laid claim to the championship, refusing to play it conservatively and merely chase points. This crew has raced for wins he went hard after Kenseth in the closing laps for a victory at Texas last week and did the same thing here.

Not comfortable settling into second place, he passed Martin Truex Jr. for the lead with 24 laps to go en route to the 33rd victory of his career and first at Phoenix.

JOHNSON AND GORDON STILL FAST FRIENDS
Homestead, Florida, Thursday, November 15, 2007

Rusty Wallace has a lot of respect for Jeff Gordon and Jimmie Johnson. But this whole friendship thing between the title contending teammates baffles the retired NASCAR champion.

"I think that's one thing to how they respect each other, but I personally think that this year's been pretty darn trying to both of them," Wallace said. "How do you treat your teammate nice and with respect, because you're wanting to kick his butt?"

Somehow, four-time champion Gordon and reigning champion Johnson have been able to draw the line between their on-track rivalry and the friendship that helped put Johnson in an elite ride at powerful Hendrick Motorsports.

It was Gordon, already established as a top star in NASCAR, who raised Johnson's name with Rick Hendrick when the car owner became serious about starting a fourth Cup team in 2001.

"The reason why I suggested Jimmie to Rick Hendrick is because he impressed me before he was ever in a Cup," explained Gordon, the co-owner of Johnson's No. 48 car with Hendrick. "I really thought if you put him in the kind of quality equipment I'd been in for all the years that he could have the same type of success that I'd had.

"It's pretty awesome to see it come from way back then to where it is now and see how he's matured."

The other half of this mutual admiration society said, "I've always, throughout my career, had someone to look up to and to learn from. At Hendrick Motorsports, Jeff is certainly that for me, and I feel that it's been good for me ... for the last five years, I've been studying Jeff and his driving styles at different tracks and, obviously, you can learn a lot from that."

The culmination of all this happy talk will come Sunday at Homestead-Miami Speedway when one of the two buddies will walk away with the Nextel Cup.

Johnson goes into the season-ending Ford 400 with a big edge four straight wins and an 86-point lead over Gordon. If Johnson finishes 18th or better, he wins the title, regardless. If Gordon finishes 15th or worse, he cedes his friend the trophy.

The two met with the media Thursday as NASCAR tried to build a little more hype for a finish that may not be as scintillating as it would like. Johnson pointed out that the friends drove to the press conference together, chatting about how well they get along despite the obvious pressures each faces.

"We are human," Johnson said. "We go through emotions and we are frustrated. We have moments where we didn't agree with what was going on out on the track, but we've always been able to talk through it, have that respect."

Wallace, the 1989 Cup champion, said it isn't really surprising how well the two native Californians get along, considering their similarities.

"They're both close to the same age," said Wallace, now an analyst for the ABC/ESPN NASCAR races. "They hang out together all the time, they have fun together, they vacation together. And they've got a great, great calming influence in their car owner that's with them all the time. This guy's at the shop all the time.

"I think they really, really respect Rick. And the things they like are almost identical."

So, do the two champions ever get annoyed with one another?

"The only thing he's irritated me with is that four (wins) in a row here lately," Gordon said, laughing. "I mean, I've got a 5.2 (finishing) average (in the Chase for the championship) and I'm 86 points down going into the final race. That irritates me."

Johnson looked a little sheepish when asked to reply to the same question.

"I really can't think of anything about Jeff that irritates me," he said, shrugging. "It is complicated and it is tough a times. But having someone you know so well and have so much respect for, I think has made it easier in our situations.

"We both have shown that we're willing to race hard and aggressive with one another."

That was most apparent in the spring race on the half-mile oval at Martinsville, where Johnson and Gordon waged a battle for the top spot over the final 53 laps, with Gordon slamming hard into Johnson's rear numerous times trying to pass before his friend held on for a narrow victory.

That kind of a duel isn't likely Sunday on the considerably faster 1.5-mile Homestead oval and Gordon has mixed emotions about trying to take the championship away from Johnson.

"We want to end the season on a positive note," Gordon said. "But the only way we're going to have a real chance is if Jimmie has a problem. We don't wish that upon anybody, and certainly not our teammate.

"I'm just proud of Hendrick Motorsports and the fact that the championship is going to come home to Rick Hendrick."

Chapter 5

PERSONAL LIFE

Winston Cup point leader Jeff Gordon and his wife Brooke look up at the timing board while on pit road awaiting Gordon's chance to qualify for the Pepsi 400 at the Daytona International Speedway, July 6, 2001. (AP Photo/Peter Cosgrove)

GORDON CONFIRMS DIVORCE FILING
Charlotte, North Carolina, Monday, March 18, 2002

Jeff Gordon confirmed Monday that his wife has filed for divorce after seven years of marriage and he asked for privacy as NASCAR's most visible couple goes through their split.

Brooke Gordon filed for divorce on Friday in Palm Beach County, Florida, saying the marriage is "irretrievably broken."

Jennifer Brooke Sealey was a Miss Winston when she met Gordon in victory lane after a race at Daytona International Speedway. Because she was forbidden to date drivers under her contract, the two met secretly for a year before she resigned her modeling position.

They married November 26, 1994, and have no children.

"I hope that everybody will respect our privacy as we work through this difficult time," Gordon said in a statement. "I also hope everybody will understand that it would be improper for me to discuss or comment on this matter publicly."

Gordon is in his 10th full season in Winston Cup. The 30-year-old driver has won four championships, 58 races and more than $45 million in prize money.

The couple has appeared in commercials and magazine stories. Brooke Gordon often signed autographs alongside her husband at events.

Gordon, off to a slow start this year in defense of his Winston Cup title, denied this weekend that personal problems have affected his on-track performance.

"My focus has been 100 percent on racing," he said.

She is seeking exclusive use of the couple's oceanfront home in Florida, valued at $9 million, as well as alimony, two cars and periodic use of their boats and an airplane.

Gordon's 32-year-old wife also wants her husband to continue to pay the salaries of their housekeepers, maintenance workers and chef, as well as her legal fees.

COUNTERSUES WIFE FOR DIVORCE
West Palm Beach, Florida, Thursday, April 11, 2002

NASCAR driver Jeff Gordon has countersued his wife for divorce, saying he should not have to equally split the couple's estate because he risked his life to collect it.

Gordon, a four-time Winston Cup champion, wants a larger share of the couple's businesses, homes, cars and boats. They have been married seven years and have no children.

"Due to the husband's extraordinary contributions to the acquisition of the funds as a result of his hazardous, life-threatening occupation, the husband claims that he should be entitled to greater than 50 percent interest in the net marital estate," according to documents filed Wednesday in Palm Beach County Circuit Court.

"He's not a banker that goes to work from 9-to-5," his divorce attorney, Donald J. Sasser, told The Palm Beach Post on Thursday. "His life is in his hands."

Gordon's wife, the former Jennifer Brooke Sealey, filed for the divorce March 15, saying the marriage is "irretrievably broken." She is seeking alimony, exclusive use of the couple's $9 million oceanfront home in Palm Beach County and periodic use of a Mercedes, Porsche, several boats and an airplane.

Her attorney, Jeff Fisher, said Jeff Gordon is "arrogant and selfish" for claiming he should get more money because his job is dangerous.

"The element of risk is irrelevant," Fisher said. "It's his choice of career."

Gordon is in his 10th full season in Winston Cup. The 30-year-old driver has won 58 races and more than $45 million in prize money.

'THE KID' NOW GOING IT ALONE
Charlotte, North Carolina, Saturday, April 20, 2002

Jeff Gordon headed for driver introductions before a recent race, fighting his way through a throng of fans.

Alone.

Joining the other drivers, he looked for a friendly face and sat down next to Ricky Craven behind the stage, laughing and joking before it was time to go to work.

For seven years, Gordon was never alone when he made this trip.

His wife, Brooke, was by his side. He usually held hands with the former Miss Winston model as they chatted in the staging area, smiling as cameras clicked away.

NASCAR's super couple.

Now, Gordon is on his own, involved in a high-profile divorce that has made as many headlines as his recent racing accomplishments.

It has given critics of the four-time Winston Cup champion a ready-made reason for his disappointing start in defending last season's title. He heads to Talladega Superspeedway this weekend eighth in the points standings with just one top-five finish for the season.

The former golden boy is not paying attention to the tabloids and the gossip - something he learned early in his career.

"My situation gives people an instant, easy excuse to point to for why I'm off to a slow start," Gordon said, lounging on the black leather couch in the back of his trailer, still wearing his flame-colored fire suit as the hum of a truck race almost drowned out his voice.

"If I wasn't going through this situation, then people wouldn't accuse me of not being focused on my job. When you get in the race car and you put that helmet on and you fire up the engine, you really don't have a choice but to be focused.

"I think that's one thing I've always been good at, whatever is going on in my life. ... I am able to do a pretty good job of putting it in the back of my mind."

By almost anyone else's standards, this season would not be so bad. He was running up front until he wrecked at Daytona and Darlington and spun out at Bristol. And he drives a Chevrolet, the only one of the four makes yet to win this year, prompting manufacturer complaints of an aerodynamic disadvantage.

But Gordon, with 58 career wins and more than $47 million in prize money, is not supposed to go 16 races without a victory - a streak dating to last season - and he's expected to finish in the top 10 every week.

Therefore, critics say, his divorce must be the first real speedbump the 30-year-old driver has faced in his decade of Winston Cup racing.

"People don't understand that every once in a while, things are going to happen in my life just like everybody else, because I'm human," he said. "Because of being in the public eye for what I do for work, when things happen to me in my personal life, it's going to make news."

For much of his career, Gordon wasn't just like everybody else.

He was too young, too handsome and too smart when he broke into Winston Cup at the age of 21 in 1992. Born in California and raised in Indiana, he didn't have the Southern background of most of his peers, didn't come up in the same ranks, didn't talk in a thick drawl.

Fans instantly hated him.

It didn't help that he was so good, winning his first race at 22 and his first title at 24 - making him the youngest Winston Cup champion ever. He doesn't understand cars, competitors said, and anyone could win with his equipment.

Finding friends was not easy for "The Kid." Earning respect was harder.

He met Jennifer Brooke Sealey, accepting a trophy from her in Victory Lane at Daytona. They saw each other secretly for a season - her contract as Miss Winston prohibited her from dating drivers - and married in 1994, a year before his first title.

They were NASCAR's superstars, appearing in commercials and magazines together. Brooke walked him to his car, was by his side in the winner's circle, was photographed as much as he was, and received just as many autograph requests as he did.

"Brooke and I had a high profile relationship and we had to," he said. "We got a lot of attention and we had to adjust our lives and what we did and how we went about it because of that."

When the fame got to be too much, they fled Charlotte - the hub of NASCAR - for a private life in Florida. There, he could slip on shorts and a baseball cap and go out for a quiet dinner with his wife.

But they were isolated in Florida and had only each other to fall back on. And his rising status in NASCAR made him standoffish and reclusive.

Gordon won't say why his marriage failed, but if there was a beginning to the end, it might have been that move in 1997.

"Moving to Florida, it was me and Brooke, we had no friends, no family," he said. "We moved away from our relationships and maybe we were a little guarded, we didn't open ourselves up to any new friends.

"Life has been good and I've been able to experience a lot of great things. But I do feel like I maybe have not been able to be myself. I had this perfect reputation and maybe I was trying to live up to that and wouldn't show that I was human."

With his private life now very public, Gordon's human side is slowly emerging. Some of it is out of his control, leaking out through court documents that show the potential for a nasty dissolution of the couple's marriage.

In filing for divorce, Brooke Gordon asked for exclusive use of their $9 million oceanfront home, alimony, two cars and periodic use of their boats and airplane. She also wants him to continue to pay the salaries of their housekeepers, maintenance workers and chef, and her legal bills.

Gordon countersued, saying he should not have to split the estate equally because he risked his life to acquire it through his hazardous profession, and he asked for a larger share of the assets.

Brooke Gordon's lawyer, Jeff Fisher, responded by calling the driver "selfish and arrogant" for claiming he deserved more because of his job.

"The element of risk is irrelevant," Fisher said last week when Gordon countersued. "It's his choice of career."

Brooke Gordon and Fisher declined to comment for this article.

Jeff Gordon said the court papers painted an incorrect picture that the split is not civil.

"I love Brooke to death, I always will. She's been my best friend for eight years," he said. "I don't like what we're going through, but I want it to come out with us being friends in the end.

"Unfortunately, you get lawyers involved and things can be a little ugly. ... To me, this is not about winning or losing, it's about moving on from the lives we had together."

So that's what Gordon is trying to do.

Regulars in the garage area have found him to be looser this season, a little more open. Gordon explains it as "coming out of my shell."

For years, Gordon refused to get too close to competitors, fearing it would be awkward if there was an on-track problem. But since word of his divorce spread last month, he's found more than one open door in the motorhome lot.

And he's repairing the friendships he ignored during his marriage.

"I feel like one thing I neglected over the last few years was friends I had for a long time or friends that I could have had, and even my family to some extent," he said. "I had a good life, one that was fulfilling in a lot of ways.

"But to be happy and balanced long term, I didn't feel like I had that, and I'm trying to fix that now."

He's also trying to get his season on track. He finished second in Texas, then won the pole last weekend at Martinsville Speedway. But he was hampered at Martinsville by a blown tire, then lost his power steering, and it required determination from him and his team just to finish 23rd.

"We've been struggling, we really have, but this team works so hard, and to finish a race like that just shows how strong we are," Gordon said. "We just have to keep digging. We're in a hole, but it's not one so deep that we can't get out of it.

"And winning cures everything."

CONFIDENTIALITY AGREEMENT
West Palm Beach, Florida, Thursday, May 9, 2002

NASCAR driver Jeff Gordon has asked that his estranged wife and anyone involved in his divorce be compelled to sign a confidentiality agreement.

Gordon contended that his employment is "highly competitive" and much of his financial information requires confidentiality, according to court documents filed in Palm Beach County Circuit Court.

Gordon wants to protect trade secrets, research and commercial information from becoming public during his divorce from Jennifer Brooke Sealey Gordon, the documents show. The confidentiality order would continue even after the divorce is final.

Circuit Judge Peter Blanc will decide in a hearing next month if the court's proceedings must remain confidential. A person at the family division of the Palm Beach County Clerk of Courts said that a notice for a June 10 confidentiality hearing was filed on May 2.

Last month, Gordon's wife twice refused to sign a confidentiality agreement.

Her lawyer, Jeff Fisher, "has adamantly refused to agree to the proposed order on confidentiality or any variation to it," according to court records.

Neither Fisher nor Donald J. Sasser, Jeff Gordon's attorney, immediately returned phone calls late Wednesday seeking comment.

The Gordons own a $9 million mansion in Highland Beach, where Gordon's wife is living. More than $40 million in assets are at stake, Jeff Gordon said a court filing.

Gordon's wife, the former Jennifer Brooke Sealey, filed for divorce March 15, saying the marriage is "irretrievably broken."

The racer countersued his wife for divorce on April 10, saying he should not have to equally split the couple's estate because he risked his life to collect it.

Gordon is winless in 11 starts in his 10th full season in Winston Cup. The 30-year-old driver has won 58 races and more than $45 million in prize money.

GORDON SPORTS GOATEE
Concord, North Carolina, Monday, May 17, 2002

A few days of not shaving got Jeff Gordon a whole lot of attention.

The four-time Winston Cup champion showed up at Lowe's Motor Speedway on Friday sporting a dark black goatee, a radical change to the clean-cut image he's presented over most of his career.

The facial hair drew a flurry of attention - cameras were constantly following him around - and he was quizzed about it every time he stopped during his preparation for The Winston, NASCAR's all-star race.

"All I wanted to do was have a little fun," said Gordon, convinced by his crew to give up shaving. "We were testing at Kansas last week and one of the guys on my team has a goatee, so they told me I should grow one, too.

"I finally told them 'What the heck, let's have a little bit of fun.' I'm enjoying it and I know the folks in the media are enjoying it, so it's pretty cool."

Gordon, who had mustache early in his career, isn't sure how long he'll keep the look.

He hasn't won in 19 races - the longest drought of his career - so if he breaks the streak in Saturday night's non-points event, he said it will stay. If he doesn't win, he plans to shave Monday morning.

The change in appearance is yet another sign of the new Gordon, who has been much looser this season even as he's going through a divorce. He's building new relationships with other drivers and is spending a lot of time with his team.

"It's all kind of funny sometimes how things work out," he said. "There are things you can do and have fun and right now that's what I want to do.

"I'm enjoying the way things are going now even though I'm not winning as much as I'm used to. I've had a great relationship with this race team in the past and they wanted to help me have a little bit of fun, so I went along with it."

GORDON WORTH $48.8 MILLION
Delray Beach, Florida, Friday, December 20, 2002

Jeff Gordon estimates he's worth about $48.8 million and earned more than $18 million in 2001, according to an affidavit filed in his divorce.

Brooke Gordon filed for a divorce in March, citing the NASCAR driver's "marital misconduct."

The racer has countersued his wife for divorce, saying he should not have to equally split the couple's estate because he risked his life to collect it.

The four-time Winston Cup champion filed the affidavit November 21 at the Palm Beach County Courthouse to comply with a Florida law that requires assets amassed during a marriage to be split evenly. He had unsuccessfully asked a judge to require his estranged wife and anyone involved in his divorce be compelled to sign a confidentiality agreement.

The statement shows that Jeff Gordon earns about $1.87 million a month - including a base salary of $29,683, bonuses of $800,000, income from other corporations and partnerships of $579,564 and income from royalties or trusts of $434,540.

After taxes, his net monthly income is $1.1 million, the affidavit shows.

Gordon lists his monthly expenses at $253,123 - including $51,903 a month to maintain his mansion on Highland Beach. He also said he donates $8,900 a month to charities.

His estranged wife has asked for exclusive use of the Highland Beach mansion, valued at $10.2 million, as well as alimony, two cars and periodic use of their boats and an airplane. She also wants her husband to continue to pay the salaries of their housekeepers, maintenance workers and chef.

Brooke Gordon was a Miss Winston when she met the driver in victory lane after a race at Daytona International Speedway.

LAWYERS TRY TO SERVE SUBPOENAS AT DAYTONA
Daytona Beach, Florida, Monday, February 10, 2003

Jeff Gordon's divorce case spilled over to the race track Monday when attorneys for his wife tried to subpoena several car owners at Daytona International Speedway.

NASCAR officials did not allow process servers into the track.

Most of the top teams have been subpoenaed at their home offices in the past month, and all have refused to open their books to Brooke Gordon and her lawyers.

Because the divorce is being heard in Florida, her lawyers want the car owners to have to fight new subpoenas in a local court.

"We wanted to take advantage of the fact they are in Florida and issue Florida subpoenas," said Terry Young, an Orlando-based attorney representing Brooke Gordon.

"If they choose to contest them, we want them to go before a Florida judge to do so."

Young said a process server was turned away Friday when NASCAR teams reported to the track to prepare for Sunday's Daytona 500, so the papers were sent again Monday with Volusia County sheriff's deputies.

Young did not know if the deputies had gotten into the track, but a NASCAR official said they did not allow the subpoenas in.

Gordon, the four-time Winston Cup champion, was aware of what was happening at the track.

"It's out of my control, but I think it's really disgusting," he said. "It's a real shame that they are trying to drag all these other guys into this because to me, there are other ways for them to get what they are looking for. This is just harassment."

The Gordons met early in the driver's career in Daytona's Victory Lane when the former Miss Winston model presented him with a trophy. They were married for seven years; she filed for divorce in March, citing marital misconduct.

Since then, her lawyers asked to examine the contracts other car owners have with their drivers and sponsors to determine what Gordon is worth as a car owner. The four-time Winston Cup champion owns a stake of Hendrick Motorsports.

NASCAR contracts are closely held secrets because teams don't want to reveal what kind of deals they are able to negotiate.

Most of the car owners have been outraged at the request to open their books, even though Jeff Fisher, Brooke Gordon's lead attorney, has promised confidentiality.

"They say they will keep it a secret, but the only way it can be kept a secret is if only two people know and one of them is dead," said car owner Felix Sabates. "This is just plain harassment, and by sending people to the race track, it shows she has no consideration for Jeff Gordon's career and thinks NASCAR is just a toy to play with."

Gordon had to turn over papers in November that estimated his worth at about $48.8 million and that he earned more than $18 million in 2001.

Brooke Gordon has asked for exclusive use of their Highland Beach, Florida, mansion, valued at $10.2 million, as well as alimony, two cars and periodic use of their boats and an airplane. She also wants him to continue to pay the salaries of their housekeepers, maintenance workers and chef.

The racer has countersued, saying he should not have to equally split the couple's estate because he risked his life to collect it.

Florida law requires assets amassed during a marriage to be split evenly.

DIVORCE SETTLEMENT
West Palm Beach, Florida, Sunday, June 15, 2003

Four-time Winston Cup champion Jeff Gordon reached a divorce settlement that guarantees his former wife at least $15.3 million.

Brooke Gordon waived alimony and will get the money from the sale of two properties, including the couple's oceanfront home in Highland Beach, according to court documents.

It was unclear when the properties would be sold or how the couple would divide other assets, which include boats, an airplane and cars.

Brooke Gordon filed for divorce in March 2002 after seven years of marriage, citing marital discord. She was "extremely pleased" with the settlement, said her lawyer, Terry Young.

Jeff Gordon also said he was happy with the terms.

In early court filings, Jeff Gordon estimated his worth at about $48.8 million and his 2001 earnings at more than $18 million.

Generally, Florida law requires assets amassed during a marriage to be split evenly, but Jeff Gordon contended he should not have to split the couple's estate because he risked his life to collect it.

GORDON MARRIES SECOND WIFE
Charlotte, North Carolina, Wednesday, November 8, 2006

Jeff Gordon took a break from the Nextel Cup championship to get married again.

The four-time NASCAR champion wed Belgian model Ingrid Vandebosch on Tuesday in a private ceremony in Mexico, Jon Edwards, Gordon's publicist, confirmed Wednesday. The wedding was first reported by Us Weekly.

NASCAR driver Jeff Gordon is cooled off by a battery-operated fan held by his fiancée Ingrid Vandebosch, left, prior to the start of the Allstate 400 at the Brickyard auto race at the Indianapolis Motor Speedway, August 6, 2006. (AP Photo/Seth Rossman)

The 35-year-old Gordon, the sport's most marketable driver, and Vandebosch have been together since 2004. They appeared in the movie "Taxi," in which the 37-year-old model played a bank robber and Gordon made an uncredited cameo appearance at her invitation.

Gordon announced his engagement to Vandebosch in Sonoma, California, in June, then won the Nextel Cup race the next day.

They began dating about a year after Gordon's much-publicized and expensive divorce from Brooke Sealy, his wife of seven years. Gordon and Brooke met in Victory Lane at Daytona International Speedway when she handed him a trophy as part of her modeling duties as a Miss Winston.

Her contract forbid her to date drivers, so the two met secretly for a year before she resigned her modeling job and married Gordon in 1994. They became NASCAR's most visible couple, and the divorce engulfed the entire garage as her lawyers tried to look at rival teams' contracts to determine Gordon's net worth. Lawyers attempted to subpoena team owners and drivers at the track during preparations for the 2003 Daytona 500.

The ordeal led to a playful pledge from Gordon that he wouldn't marry again until his driving career was over.

Vandebosch, who began modeling at age 12, according to an online biography, has also dated former Baltimore Orioles star Brady Anderson.

Gordon recently surpassed $80 million in career winnings. He's competing for a fifth Cup championship and is sixth in the standings entering this weekend's race at Phoenix International Raceway.

FATHERHOOD
Birmingham, Alabama, Wednesday, March 28, 2007

This much Jeff Gordon knows for sure: His life will change dramatically when his daughter is born this summer.

And maybe, just maybe, his NASCAR career won't seem quite so important.

"I think it's going to be one of two things: It's either going to make me work that much harder and appreciate racing that much more and enjoy it that much more," Gordon said. "Or it's going to make me go, 'I don't even want to do this.'"

The prospect of fatherhood the baby is due in late June or early July certainly hasn't diminished his enthusiasm for racing. The four-time Cup champion is off to a career-best start and leading the points race for the first time since February 2005.

The 35-year-old Gordon is fresh off a third-place finish at Bristol Motor Speedway, his third top-5 already this season.

"I think that our team is really strong right now," said Gordon, seeking his first Cup title since 2001. "Every time we go through something like we went through Sunday, where we faded to the back and fought our way to the front, it only makes us stronger."

More than a few skeptics wondered whether Gordon's off-the-track good fortune his November marriage to supermodel Ingrid Vandebosch and then the news of the baby would have the opposite effect.

Crew chief Steve Letarte, however, is convinced the baby will be a blessing for Gordon on and off the track.

"He's lived for this sport. When he has a chance to go home and hold his little girl and have time to spend with his wife, I think that puts it all in perspective," said Letarte, who has two young children. "I think it's going to help us. I think it's going to be the best thing ever."

Jimmie Johnson, the reigning Nextel Cup champion and Gordon's teammate, agreed.

"There are a lot of people who have started families and had successful families and racing careers," Johnson said. "Jeff Gordon is one of the best on the track, and I don't see it changing him."

Gordon happily admitted he has trouble imagining the changes a baby will bring. Maybe he should compare notes with Tiger Woods, also awaiting his first child.

Gordon said he and Woods, an acquaintance, haven't discussed impending fatherhood, but he figured things won't be the same.

"He won't be the same golfer. I guarantee you I won't be the same race car driver," Gordon said. "That doesn't mean the results are going to be bad, though. I can't really answer that question until it comes. I think it's going to put a lot of things in perspective for me."

Gordon acknowledged any post-birth struggles on the track likely will be linked to being a distracted dad.

"If my performance falls off for any reason, I think that's going to be the first thing that's going to pop up," Gordon said. "That's expected. It's a story."

But how can a guy with nearly $85 million in career earnings, a supermodel bride, a baby on the way and a Cup series lead complain?

"It can be very easy to forget how good you've got it," Gordon said. "I try to remind myself as often as I can and I tell other people around me: Don't forget to remind me that life is good."

BABY GIRL
New York, Wednesday, June 20, 2007

Jeff Gordon won't have to miss a race for the birth of his daughter.

NASCAR's four-time champion became a father Wednesday when his wife, model Ingrid Vandebosch, gave birth to a girl. Gordon announced on his Web site that Ella Sofia Gordon was born Wednesday morning.

"It's been an absolutely incredible experience," Gordon said. "Ingrid came through amazingly and we're both really happy and overjoyed. We can't wait to get home and start our lives together as a family."

Gordon asked Mark Martin to be on standby this weekend in case he had to leave the race in Sonoma, California, to return for the birth. He said he'll travel to California later this week and participate in all on-track activities at Infineon Raceway.

Gordon's baby was born two days after Tiger Woods' daughter.

LIFE'S GOOD
Charlotte, North Carolina, Saturday, June 23, 2007

Jeff Gordon helicoptered into the race track, escorted four friends to his motorhome and instructed them where they could find food and beer. Then he slid into the back of a waiting SUV set to shuttle him to a full schedule of pre-race appearances. The buzzing of his cell phone interrupted his conversation, as Gordon fumbled to answer it quickly.

"Hey, baby," he cooed to his wife, Belgian model Ingrid Vandebosch, "I miss you.'"

Gordon's personal life has never been better, and his professional life is on track for a fifth NASCAR championship. With the
addition of his first child Ella Sofia was born Wednesday Gordon
now must figure out how to juggle both.

"You are now responsible for this little person that can't take
care of itself," Carol Bickford, his mother, said. "And how is he going
to do that and race, too? Well you know what? We all have jobs. We
all have kids, and we all find a way to work, too.

"We all do it. He'll do the same thing."

NASCAR's newest daddy goes back to work this weekend in
Sonoma, California, where he'll try for his fifth victory of the season.
He'll leave his girls behind in New York City, the first test of how he
handles being a famous race car driver and a family man.

After all, racing is no longer the most important thing in his
life.

"After winning the four championships and as many races as
he has, he doesn't feel like he's got anything to prove to anyone,"
said car owner Rick Hendrick. "I just think the baby and Ingrid
mean so much more to him than trying to prove to anybody that
he's the man."

The Nextel Cup Series has 22 fathers who are raising children
while racing cars every weekend. Some had their kids before they
made it big; others started their families well into their NASCAR
careers.

None are as a big a star as Gordon, the four-time series champion and Madison Ave. pitchman who has been through several
cycles of highs and lows during his 15 years on top of the sport.

He's racked up 79 victories best among active drivers, sixth on
the all-time list and a NASCAR-record $85 million in winnings. He
had a high-profile first marriage to Brooke Sealy, a former series
model, and a much-publicized and expensive divorce seven years
later.

He spent time isolated in Florida, away from the day-to-day
NASCAR grind and out of the public spotlight, and distanced himself from his parents during the bulk of his first marriage.

Those who know him insist that through every twist and turn,
Gordon has always been 100 percent committed to his craft.

"When he shows up in this garage, I don't think there's ever
been a moment that he's not been prepared," said crew chief Steve

Letarte. "Over 15 years of knowing him, he's always shown up ready to do his job. He's always on his A-game."

That hasn't changed since Gordon met Vandebosch in 2004. The two announced their engagement the morning of the Sonoma race last year and were married in Mexico in early November. They announced they were expecting a month later.

Although the relationship hasn't changed him, he appears to finally be content. Now 35, Gordon's mother says he's finally comfortable in his skin.

Gordon has been unstoppable this year in the best statistical start of his career. He's got four wins and 13 top-10 finishes through 15 races. He also has such a comfortable lead atop the points standings that he would have missed the first race of his career if Vandebosch had gone into labor this weekend.

It's a return to form after several lean years following his fourth title in 2001. After missing the Chase for the championship in 2004 a shocking failure for a driver who had not been outside the top 10 in points since his 1993 rookie season last season was the start of his comeback. He got a pair of wins and a Chase berth. But Gordon never got rolling once the postseason started, and he finished a distant sixth as teammate Jimmie Johnson won his first title.

Gordon believes this season's success is a direct correlation to the satisfaction of his personal life.

"I always had hoped that there was going to be a day in my life that things were going really good in my relationships. There is nothing better than sharing those winning moments and success with the people you care about the most, and I've never before had it all," Gordon said. "If you go back to my first championship, I was recently married and happy. But my mom and dad, we went through our problems, and they weren't a part of it. As happy as I was, I was not happy about that situation.

"So it seems like there's always going to be something. But right now, I can't think of anything major not going well."

It raises questions about how long Gordon plans to run the grueling 36-race schedule. He's adamant he wants to be a hands-on father and has spent the past nine months at doctor appointments, baby showers, assembling furniture and researching strollers he wanted "sleek, lightweight, safe and cool" and settled on a pair of $900 prams.

He views raising a child as the most important job he'll ever have. Because he doesn't want to be an absentee father, Gordon plans to have Ingrid and Ella on the road with him as much as possible.

The problem is, his at-track schedule is stacked with appearances, appointments and entertaining. When he finally returns to the motorhome at the end of a long day, Gordon needs rest and relaxation, and a baby could disrupt that downtime.

"Ingrid doesn't want to do that to me while I am at the races; she knows how important those weekends are," Gordon said. "And as much as I'd like to visit and spend time, if it's going to be disruptive, then it's not worth it."

So for now, the two won't travel with him. The family plans to use a baby nurse to help put Ella on a schedule. When she starts coming to the race track, they'll have a new motorhome equipped with a built-in crib and playpen.

It might make other crew chiefs worry that their driver won't be focused come race day, but Letarte isn't too concerned.

"Maybe that kid keeping him up all night he'll want to get in a race car, it will at least be quiet," Letarte said. "But it's certainly not going to lessen his drive. Every part of his life is complete, and I think there's nothing more that he wants than to take Ingrid to New York as a champion and carry his baby around New York as the champion.

"He's at the point of his career where this is all about putting his name down as the champion at the end of this special year."

Still, Gordon isn't sure what to expect the next few months. He doesn't know how his baby will change his life, and a part of him fears the unknown.

"Everything scares me about fatherhood, and the thing that scares me the most is failure," he said. "I think it's the toughest job on the planet, and I am sure it's going to change me. But I hope it's going to change me in a positive way, and not a negative way.

"My career is extremely important. But I want to be a great father, and I just don't know if anything is going to be more important than my child."

SECOND CHILD
Daytona Beach, Florida, Thursday, February 4, 2010

Four-time NASCAR champion Jeff Gordon is getting ready to become a father for the second time.

He made the announcement on his Web site Thursday, then confirmed it at Daytona 500 media day. Gordon says his wife, Ingrid, is 12 weeks pregnant. Their first child, Ella, will be 3 in June.

Gordon joins a growing list of NASCAR drivers expecting children this season. Four-time defending Sprint Cup champion Jimmie Johnson and his wife are expecting their first child in July.

Carl Edwards and Elliott Sadler could become first-time fathers any day. Both their wives are due early this month. And Juan Pablo Montoya and his wife are expecting their third child in July.

Jeff Gordon with daughter Ella Sofia and wife Ingrid at the NASCAR Daytona 500 auto race, February 14, 2010. (AP Photo/J Pat Carter)

BIG PAPA
New York, Saturday, May 29, 2010

Papa pulls his oversized SUV along an Upper West Side curb on a cold, wet weekday and makes one last check to be sure the back seat entertainment system is working. Then he zigzags his way through raindrops, nannies and strollers toward the preschool entrance.

Ten minutes later, he emerges in a full-on sprint with the love of his life, a blonde 2-year-old. If he stays on schedule, they'll have

30 precious minutes together for books and games before he heads to work.

"Come see my playroom!" little Ella shrieks as she bounced through the door of their apartment.

Papa is more commonly known as Jeff Gordon, NASCAR's four-time champion and all-time earnings leader at $111 million in race winnings. He's the superstar who transformed stock-car racing on and off the track. His 82 career victories rank fifth-most in history, and he's credited with forever changing the moneymaking prospects for drivers. He spent his childhood perfecting the polish and charm that dazzled Madison Avenue and opened opportunities never before seen in NASCAR.

But here, sitting cross-legged on the floor of an apartment that if it were any closer to Central Park it would actually be in the famous green space, he's just Papa.

"I love being a dad. It's the greatest," he said. "It's changed how I go about day to day, and what's important to me. Every day is, 'How she's doing? What's new? What can I teach her? What am I not teaching her?'"

Gordon, who will turn 39 in August, has reinvented himself for at least the third time in his professional career. Now he's a family guy. And the funny thing is, despite all the warnings that fatherhood would ruin his competitive spirit, it's actually making him more fiery on the track.

He was a 20-year-old with a mustache and a mullet on the fast track to superstardom when he broke into NASCAR's elite Cup division in the 1992 season finale. He made his debut the same day seven-time champion Richard Petty took his final bow, and the symbolic changing of the guard was lost on no one.

By the time Gordon won his first race, the 1994 Coca-Cola 600, he was clean-shaven and cried from the cockpit of a car he'd named "Brooke" after his then-fiancée, Brooke Sealey. He married the former Victory Lane model soon after, and the couple morphed into the "Ken and Barbie" of NASCAR.

They were squeaky clean, charitable and deeply religious. Gordon spoke at Promise Keeper conventions, and the couple held Bible studies in their home. But the push for perfection took its toll on the couple and Gordon says now that he knew the marriage was over during the trophy presentation at Atlanta in 2001 for his fourth championship.

NASCAR drivers Dale Earnhardt, driving the GM Goodwrench Chevrolet, from Kannapolis, North Carolina, left, and Jeff Gordon, driving the Dupont Chevrolet, from Pittsboro, Tennessee, watch qualifying at Daytona International Speedway, July 1, 1993. (AP Photo/Peter Cosgrove)

Divorce proceedings began early in 2002, and with them came a brand new Gordon.

As a single, he began to live a less-guarded life. There were parties, nightclubs, models, a guest host gig on "Saturday Night Live" and a newfound love of New York City, which had admittedly intimidated him most of his life.

Gordon also had himself a wingman in Jimmie Johnson, the protégé he'd brought to Hendrick Motorsports the year before. The two were close, sometimes inseparable, as they racked up wins and celebrated their fame together.

But people change over time, and Gordon and Johnson eventually settled down. For Gordon, his new love was a Belgian model named Ingrid Vandebosch, who had spurned him a few years earlier when, fresh off his divorce, he refused to commit to a serious relationship.

Given a second chance with the leggy brunette, he fell head over heels in love and the two were married late in the 2006 season.

Their first child, Ella Sofia, was born the next June and so began Gordon's third makeover.

As Gordon heads into Sunday's 16th anniversary of his first career victory, he opened up his life to The Associated Press and USA Today, inviting both media outlets to spend a week with the driver known simply as "Four-Time" throughout the industry. He granted access to appearances, meetings, a weekly conference call with his HMS teammates and family time.

His first day in New York began with an appearance for ESPN and a brief meet-and-greet with Disney CEO Bob Iger and ESPN president George Bodenheimer. There's just enough time to go home and change out of his suit before it's time to pick up Ella, whom the Gordons are raising with the help of a part-time nanny. Ella wants to play and read and show the guests her bedroom, but Papa has only a limited amount of time before his weekly HMS conference call.

Lunch is in the lobby restaurant of his building, where he cuts Ella's salmon and feeds it to her while imploring her to "sit like a lady" or else no dessert. Then it's off to his workout, a trek that takes two different trains but Gordon remains blissfully anonymous in the crowded subway.

The most striking part of Gordon's week, though, is the family time. He crams in every 30 minutes he can while splitting time between New York City and Charlotte, N.C., where he's in the final stages of building a home for Ingrid and the kids. Their second child, a boy, is due in August.

His daughter has made him more aware of what's important and how he wants her to view him. With just one points win since 2008 a race at Texas last season that Ella missed Gordon has yet to celebrate with his daughter in Victory Lane and it gnaws at him.

"I really feel my work is almost more important to me now because it almost has more purpose and meaning," he said. "I think I kind of lost that a little bit. OK, I want to win and get a trophy and make money, but what does that really mean? Now my pride is on the line.

"I don't want her walking on the bus mentioning any other driver's name. 'Yeah Papa! Way to go!' I want to make her proud."

This could be the year.

After two sub-par seasons, Gordon is back on his game. Although he's yet to reach Victory Lane in 2010 he's stuck in a 42-race winless streak he's led a Sprint Cup Series-best 709 laps and has been in position to win four times.

As team owner Rick Hendrick noted, Gordon is "on the chip. He's fired up. He's kind of getting in his groove. I see so much of the old Jeff."

Gordon won't admit that the fire was ever gone, or that jealousy over Johnson's four-consecutive titles and 17 wins over the last two years has spurred him to turn it up a notch.

Instead, he points to better cars from crew chief Steve Letarte as the reason for his resurgence.

"When you don't run good, it takes a lot out of you," he said simply. "I know that when the cars are right, the fire will be there. Fire doesn't make the car go faster. Desire doesn't make the car go faster. That's the only difference I've seen this year."

But that's not entirely true.

Gordon and Letarte went winless in 2008, then finished a distant third in the standings to teammates Johnson and Mark Martin in last year's one-win season. Afterward, the two had some very candid conversations about the direction of the No. 24 team.

Gordon characterized the talks as a heart-to-heart intended to improve communication. "We need to be better than this. I know we're better than this," Gordon recalled. But Letarte paints a heavier picture.

"Jeff and I had a lot of heated discussions all winter long of whether I'm the guy, or whether he wants to be the guy, and how devoted do we want to be? Where is our commitment?" Letarte said. "We are big boys and we have never held back from one another, so we sat back and put it all on the table and didn't hold anything back.

"I think without a doubt we've shown each other how committed we are to this race team. And since Daytona, I have no doubt in my mind that when we start each Sunday, he wants it as bad or worse as anybody on the race track."

Part of Gordon's recommitment comes from improved physical condition as he's recovered from back pain he suffered through during the last two seasons. When no treatment seemed to help his aching back, Gordon finally heeded his wife's advice to see trainer David Kirsch of Madison Square Club.

Kirsch had helped Ingrid prepare for a Sports Illustrated swimsuit shoot four months after giving birth, and his hour-long circuit training sessions helped Gordon's back.

"Jeff today versus Jeff a year ago is night and day," Kirsch said. "He wasn't in terrible shape. He wasn't overweight. His back was an issue. There was genuine concern with what was going on with his lower spine, and we were able to avoid (surgery) through his workouts."

The sessions, sometimes as many as three times a week and sometimes not at all because of Gordon's schedule, have helped the driver both on and off the track.

"His confidence and his swagger are both improved," Kirsch said. "When you look and feel good, there's no words for that. I know he gets into the car knowing he's as physically prepared as his car is prepared."

Gordon, who admits to an increased tolerance for the aches, believes he's in the best shape of his life and poised to finally finish the "Drive for Five" campaign that began in 2001, two reinventions ago long before diapers, play dates and a chance for Papa to make his baby girl proud.

"Things are going well and we're backing it up with communication, physical fitness, good cars, good teamwork," Gordon said. "But right now, this team feels if the Chase started tomorrow, we'd have a hell of a shot at the championship."

Chapter 6

FIERY SIDE

Jeff Gordon talks to reporters after a crash and altercation with Jeff Burton during the NASCAR Sprint Cup Series auto race at Texas Motor Speedway, November 7, 2010. (AP Photo/Tim Sharp)

GORDON SHOVES BURTON IN TEXAS TANGLE
Fort Worth, Texas, Sunday, November 7, 2010

An angry Jeff Gordon hit Jeff Burton with a hard two-handed push after Burton sent Gordon's car crashing into the outside wall during a caution period Sunday.

After getting out of his No. 24 car, Gordon walked from the top to the bottom of the track to confront Burton. Gordon shoved Burton, then took some swings before they were separated by two NASCAR safety officials.

"Thankfully, I had a long walk to him down the backstretch because I did about the least amount I was going to. I wanted to do a whole lot more to him," Gordon said. "You know, I like Jeff, he's a guy that's usually very rational and I respect his opinion and he apologized, said it was his fault, said he didn't mean to do it, and whatever. It's over."

The drivers then rode together in ambulance to the infield-care center.

"I didn't want to be in the ambulance with him," Gordon said. "I'll tell you that."

Burton took full responsibility for the accident "100 percent, it was my fault," he said and had no problem with what Gordon did.

"I don't blame him for being mad. I would have been mad too," Burton said.

Right before the caution came out for another problem on the track, Burton said he came down from a higher groove in Turn 4 and that Gordon had to drive under him. It was difficult to see on that part of the track because of the setting sun.

When a caution then came out for more problems on Martin Truex Jr.'s car, Gordon initially drove up beside Burton and then drove away.

Burton said he was then trying to catch up with Gordon to acknowledge his mistake. But as he came up from behind in Turn 2, their cars hit and crashed.

"Honestly, I don't know what happened," Burton said. "I didn't mean to wreck him. ... I don't have a bit of a problem with what he did. We talked. He's still upset. I don't blame him."

Gordon said he never expected anything like that to happen between he and Burton.

"I lost a lot of respect for him," Gordon said.

With Gordon out of the race, the Hendrick team moved Gordon's pit crew to the No. 48 of points leader Jimmie Johnson, who had lost spots on the track because of several slow stops.

CREW CHIEFS TRADE BARBS
Charlotte, North Carolina, Wednesday, November 10, 2010

The animosity on pit road began five weeks ago, when Jimmie Johnson's team broke an unwritten code by selecting the stall right in front of Denny Hamlin.

Championship contenders traditionally stay away from each other on pit road, and Hamlin crew chief Mike Ford was none too pleased by the lack of respect from Johnson crew chief Chad Knaus. Turnabout is fair play, though, and Ford repaid the slight last weekend at Texas Motor Speedway by selecting the pit stall in front of Johnson.

Then, when Johnson's pit crew struggled through some early stops that ultimately led to their benching, Ford couldn't help but wonder if the pressure of watching the flawless execution of Hamlin's crew a few feet away didn't play a part in their problems.

"You put the two pit crews toe-to-toe and those guys are going to make mistakes," Ford boasted after Hamlin's win Sunday at Texas pushed the No. 11 team past Johnson and into the points lead.

"We went beside them, and those guys faltered, and it made them panic and push to the point where they made changes."

Knaus benched his crew midway through Sunday's race after Hendrick Motorsports teammate Jeff Gordon crashed, and his crew became available for the rest of the day. The swap became official this week when HMS said Gordon's crew would pit Johnson for the final two races in the Chase for the Sprint Cup championship, in which Johnson trails Hamlin by 33 points.

So, did Hamlin and Ford and the FedEx team really get inside the heads of Johnson's crew to the point they couldn't perform at Texas? And, will mind games and mental warfare play a factor in deciding this championship?

Veteran driver Jeff Burton thinks the issue is black and white and a sports psychologist isn't needed to decipher the performance issues.

"I think a lot of people take a lot of credit for things that perhaps were just coincidence," Burton said. "But the 48 has not had typical 48 pit stops for a large part of the year. This wasn't the first race they've had a problem. If this was the first race they've had a problem then maybe (Ford) could make that case.

"But this isn't the first race they haven't been as good as you would expect them to be."

The fact is, of the three championship contenders, it's widely believed that Johnson's pit crew has been the weakest even though he's the four-time defending champion. Through attrition, promotion or being lured away by other teams, the core seven over-the-wall guys has changed from Johnson's first championship to the group that was benched Sunday.

Still, it took 34 races for Knaus to make a change, and when he did in the middle of the race, Ford viewed it as a "desperation move."

Knaus pleaded ignorance on the slight "my plate's been pretty full," he said but denied Ford's claim that his team is better than the four-time defending champion's.

"I don't know that they're a better team by any means," Knaus said. "It's funny that they're more worried about us than worried about themselves. I think I would be worried about focusing on that 11 car instead of the 48. "

That line of thinking has helped Johnson to his four titles. Not since losing to Tony Stewart in 2005 has Johnson worried about the competition, focusing instead on what he and the No. 48 team have to achieve each week.

It's hard to tell if Hamlin's group is subscribing to that theory. While the words flying back and forth between each team would seem to indicate a level of gamesmanship not seen in NASCAR in over a decade, both teams denied being worried about the other.

Knaus dismissed Ford's notion that the crew swap was done because it's more important for Hendrick to win as a company than as an individual team.

"Obviously, that's not a very good team over there then. If we start to think about the individuals here, we don't operate as a team. Especially in this building, we're thick as thieves," Knaus said about the shop that both Johnson's and Gordon's teams work from.

Ford insisted his assessments aren't a bid to mess with the champions.

"Mind games only work if you let them," Ford said. "And if you get all caught up trying to mess with people, you lose sight of what you are supposed to be doing."

With two races to go including Phoenix, where Johnson has won four of the last six races it's clear both teams are looking for every edge they can find.

PIT SELECTONS DRAW CROWD AT PHOENIX
Avondale, Arizona, Saturday, November 13, 2010

The drama began shortly after the garage at Phoenix International Raceway opened Saturday and crew chiefs began to ponder what pit stall they'd select for the Sprint Cup race.

The weekly process usually goes off with zero fanfare. But since crew chiefs Chad Knaus and Mike Ford turned pit selection into an integral part of the championship race, Saturday's pick session turned into an event.

"Where were you guys at Kansas?" Ford asked the media gathered around a garage stall where a NASCAR official moderates the picks.

The entire affair goes back to the September race at Kansas, where Denny Hamlin crew chief Ford complained that Knaus broke an unwritten code by selecting the spot in front of them for Jimmie Johnson.

Ford got his revenge last week in Texas by selecting the stall in front of Johnson, and some believe it contributed to the poor performance from Johnson's crew that led to their midrace benching.

So the wait was on to see if the three championship contenders would choose stalls near each other in Sunday's race. Picking order is determined by qualifying, and since Hamlin was the highest qualifier of the three, Ford went first.

He took spot 18, which had open slots in front and behind, then waited to see what the competition would do. Knaus got his turn three picks later, and chose to go to the back of pit road, far away from Hamlin, in spot 39.

Drama denied.

Or was it?

As the process played out, Ford soon found himself blocked in by the teammates of the championship contenders. Dale Earnhardt Jr., a teammate of Johnson's, was given the spot in front of Hamlin, while Kevin Harvick teammate Jeff Burton got the slot behind Hamlin.

Either driver could make getting in and out of the pits difficult for Hamlin on Sunday.

Johnson and Harvick are in much better shape.

Harvick has Dave Blaney in the spot in front of him, and if Blaney attempts to run the entire race, he'll likely not be on the lead lap and thus won't be on pit road at the same time as Harvick.

Bobby Labonte has the pit stall between Johnson and Harvick, and Paul Menard has the stall behind Johnson.

Based on past performance, there's a solid chance Harvick won't have cars surrounding him on the lead lap or in the pits for much of the race.

NOT BUDGING: Even after a civil conversation with Jeff Burton about their accident under caution at Texas, Jeff Gordon is not accepting the explanation he was given.

"I'm never going to agree with what went on at Texas," Gordon said. "We had a good conversation. I have a lot of respect and I always have and I may have lost some for him, but I still really respect him. It was stupid what he did. You can't get in behind a guy and get caught up in it yourself. That's the part that I'll never understand.

"I told him, 'I will never understand how I got wrecked under caution and how you got caught up in it at the same time.' If you are going to wreck somebody, it's easy to do and usually pretty easy to stay out of it yourself."

Gordon drove alongside Burton under caution to show his displeasure over how Burton had raced him moments earlier. Seconds later. Burton turned Gordon and both cars hit the wall.

Burton has insisted he wasn't trying to wreck Gordon on purpose.

"I went to let him know, 'Hey, I got it,' but also I didn't understand why he was as mad as he seemed to be," Burton said. "That was just frustration. Then the rest of it was just I honestly don't know how to explain what happened after that, I really don't. That is really it."

The drivers scuffled after the race as a furious Gordon charged after Burton and gave him a hard two-handed shove. They were locked up for a moment before a pair of NASCAR officials stepped in.

"I didn't punch him, we shoved, we shouted and we got our frustration out, but we didn't cross over the line, either one of us, in my opinion," Gordon said.

The scrap earned Gordon some ribbing at last week's Country Music Awards, where he was a presenter.

"How about ol' scrappy here this weekend," country music star Brad Paisley said to him. "You want to lay one on me?"

"I'll take you down, man," Gordon said.

EDWARDS ON TOP: Carl Edwards will try to snap his 70-race winless streak Sunday at Phoenix, where he's dominated every on-track session leading into the race.

Edwards set a track record in winning the pole, and paced all three practice sessions.

"This is the fastest car we've had for a long time and it's nice," he said. "I like it a lot. Hopefully, we can run well on the long run because that's going to be the true test. I feel like we're pretty decent and now we just have to go do it."

Edwards has not won a Cup race since the 2008 season finale at Homestead.

BABY WATCH: Ryan Newman is the latest driver in limbo he's awaiting the birth of his first child, and needs a standby driver just in case the moment comes when he's behind the wheel.

Krissie Newman is expecting the birth of the couple's daughter on November 26, and didn't make the trip to Phoenix. Ron Hornaday is the standby driver, and turned some laps in Saturday's final practice as a precautionary measure.

Asked what he'll do if he gets the call from home during the race, Newman didn't sound entirely committed to getting out of the car.

"Honestly, I don't know. It all depends on the timing of things," he said. "Obviously, if I am in the car, another few laps may not hurt. I'm just saying. I have a couple people in line to delay the message as it gets to me, just in case.

"Obviously, that is really important in my life. Our first baby. I don't know if you can say first baby or last baby or whatever, but, it is important to be there. To be there for her."

GORDON FINED $100K AND DOCKED 25 POINTS
Charlotte, North Carolina, Tuesday, November 13, 2010

Four-time NASCAR champion Jeff Gordon avoided suspension Monday when NASCAR instead fined him $100,000 and docked him 25 points for intentionally wrecking Clint Bowyer at Phoenix International Raceway.

Gordon also was placed on probation through December 31. But he'll be allowed to close out the season at Homestead-Miami Speedway despite his actions in Sunday's race, which triggered a fight in the garage area between the two drivers' crews.

"I take responsibility for my actions on the racetrack," Gordon said in a statement. "I accept NASCAR's decision and look forward to ending the season on a high note at Homestead."

The penalty drops Gordon to 11th in the Chase for the Sprint Cup championship with one race remaining. He's now four points behind Martin Truex Jr. for 10th, and only the top-10 drivers have formal roles in the season-ending awards ceremony in Las Vegas.

Rick Hendrick also was docked 25 car owner points, and crew chief Alan Gustafson was placed on probation through the end of the year.

"I've always respected Jeff for standing his ground," said Hendrick, owner of Hendrick Motorsports. "We also respect that NASCAR needs to police the sport and send a message when situations like this occur. It's been a great year, and we're going to put our focus on finishing in a positive way this weekend."

Gordon intentionally slowed his car and waited for Bowyer on the track Sunday to wreck him on what was scheduled to be the final lap. There had been contact between the two a few laps earlier, and Gordon viewed it as the final straw in an apparently escalating on-track feud with Bowyer.

He said after the incident he was "fed up" with Bowyer, and had to take a stand Sunday and would wait to see how NASCAR responded.

"They've got to do what they've got to do, and I guess I had to do what I had to do," he said.

The accident collected Joey Logano and Aric Almirola, and happened right in front of championship contender Brad Keselowski, who had to weave his way around the carnage.

It also led to the brawl in the garage that began when Gordon appeared to be jumped from behind by a Michael Waltrip Racing team member. Gordon was grabbed by a Hendrick Motorsports crew member and pulled out of the fracas and into his team hauler.

Bowyer, bewildered to find his stall empty when his burning race car came to a stop on pit road, saw the fight on the infield big screen and sprinted over the wall and through the garage to back up his guys. He was held back by NASCAR officials from entering Gordon's hauler.

Bowyer crew chief Brian Pattie was fined $25,000 and placed on probation through the end of the year for failing to maintain control of the crew.

NASCAR vice president of competition Robin Pemberton considered the matter closed after issuing the penalties.

"There's no doubt that a unique set of circumstances combined with a championship battle on the line resulted in raw emotions coming into play," he said. "We consider the penalties appropriate and those involved understand our decision and we expect them to abide by them."

And Michael Waltrip Racing apologized for the actions of its crew members, which said they did not live up to the standards it has set for its race team but was sparked because the accident "brought raw emotions of a long and hard championship battle to the surface."

Bowyer could have climbed back into the championship battle on Sunday, but Gordon's actions instead dropped him to fourth in the standings and mathematically eliminated him from title contention.

Meanwhile, Keselowski was fined $25,000 and placed on probation for having an electronic device inside the car the phone he used to tweet during a red flag period caused by Gordon wrecking Bowyer.

Keselowski first tweeted during a red flag at the season-opening Daytona 500, and he was widely celebrated for his social media usage. He posted his view of the jet fuel fire that stopped the race for over two hours, answered questions and gave updates during the first prime-time Daytona 500 in history.

But NASCAR later told teams they could not have electronic devices in their cars, even though Keselowski has tweeted without penalty from Victory Lane at Bristol and from inside his car during a rain delay at Richmond since Daytona. It had some fans wondering Monday if he was really being penalized for a profanity-laced answer he gave during Sunday's post-race news conference about the race.

Keselowski was upset about what he believed was a double standard from drivers who had been critical a week earlier of how aggressive he had raced Jimmie Johnson on a pair of restarts at Texas. He argued with colorful language that it didn't come close to the Gordon-Bowyer incident on Sunday, or the last-lap crash that occurred because NASCAR failed to throw a caution despite oil on the track.

"It's the double standard that I spent a whole week being bashed by a half-dozen drivers about racing hard at Texas and how I'm out of control and have a death wish," he said. "These guys just tried to kill each other ... they should be ashamed. It's embarrassing."

GRUDGE DATES BACK 7 MONTHS
Homestead, Florida, Saturday, November 17, 2012

When Clint Bowyer and Jeff Gordon made contact in the closing laps at Phoenix, Gordon was overcome by a grudge he'd been carrying at least seven months.

The four-time NASCAR champion retaliated by intentionally wrecking Bowyer, triggering a garage-area melee.

Clint Bowyer's pit crew pushes his car into the garage area after a crash with Jeff Gordon during the NASCAR Sprint Cup Series auto race at Phoenix International Raceway, November 11, 2012. (AP Photo/Ross D. Franklin)

Gordon's reputation took a hit among his peers and he was fined $100,000 by NASCAR. But he avoided suspension and will race Sunday in the season finale at Homestead-Miami Speedway, where he'll celebrate his 20th anniversary with sponsor DuPont and Hendrick Motorsports.

He admitted Friday that DuPont had initial concerns NASCAR would park him this weekend for his actions Sunday at Phoenix, but he never worried he wouldn't race at Homestead and he's not sorry for wrecking Bowyer.

"The thing that I regret and the thing that I messed up on is that I allowed my anger and my emotions to put me in a position to make a bad choice," Gordon said. "I felt like Clint needed to be dealt with, but that wasn't the right way to go about it, certainly not the right time. And what I hate most about it is that other guys were involved with it and it affected their day."

The wreck collected Joey Logano and Aric Almirola, and championship points leader Brad Keselowski had to dodge his way around the accident scene. It also triggered a brawl in the garage between Gordon's crew and Bowyer's crew that has received as much attention as the championship race between Keselowski and five-time NASCAR champion Jimmie Johnson.

It has also thrust the 41-year-old Gordon into the headlines at the end of yet another disappointing season.

He was docked 25 points for Sunday's bad behavior, which dropped him to 11th in the Sprint Cup Series standings in this one-win season. He hasn't won a championship since 2001, and teammate Johnson, who came on board in 2002, will race for his sixth title Sunday.

So his actions on Sunday were certainly that of a frustrated driver, and he admitted wrecking Bowyer sent a message to the garage.

"I don't think they're going to be messing with me for a little while. I think they realize that that message was sent pretty clear," Gordon said. "Throughout the last couple years, I feel like one thing that maybe I haven't done enough of is show the fire inside me that I have to want to win and want to win championships. And I think that while I would have liked to have gone about it differently on Sunday, I think it did show that that fire and passion is inside of me in a big way."

So big that he'd been angry with Bowyer since Martinsville in April, when Bowyer played a role in costing Hendrick Motorsports its 200th victory.

The race had been dominated that day by Gordon and Johnson, and a late caution had set up a restart with the teammates lined up side-by-side at the front. Bowyer re-started in the second row, on new tires, and got a shove from behind from Ryan Newman. He dove to the inside of Gordon and Johnson, made contact, and all three wrecked.

It was a crushing defeat for the Hendrick camp, which was moments away from celebrating a historic victory at Martinsville, site of some of the team's most significant triumphs and its most heartbreaking tragedy. A Hendrick plane crashed en route to a 2004 race at Martinsville, among the 10 people on board were Hendrick's brother, son, twin nieces, key team personnel and a DuPont representative.

At the April race with Hendrick, for the first time since the 2004 plane crash, were the widows of Hendrick's brother and the DuPont executive.

"We were all wanting to win more than anything, more than any championship. The 200th win at Martinsville meant so much to all of us because we lost so much there," Hendrick said Friday. "And that was taken away from us. Both of our cars were wrecked on the last lap and next to last lap and it was by the 15 car (Bowyer). I have never hurt as bad in my life leaving the race track as I did that day. It took me a week or so to get over it just because we had it in our grasp. And that's just emotions that we carry and nobody else. So I think that situation, along with some other things that happened along the way, you know, you don't forget it."

Bowyer and Gordon spoke at the track that day, and Bowyer texted Hendrick after the race. The two drivers have had other on-track incidents between them this season, including another run-in at Martinsville last month, but they had a conversation after that, too.

But something made Gordon snap late in Sunday at Phoenix, when enough was finally enough when he and Bowyer got together. When Gordon retaliated, it mathematically eliminated Bowyer from championship contention, but Gordon said Bowyer has to accept responsibility for putting himself in that position.

"If you're contending for the championship, you've got to be as smart about the things you do on the race track as the guys that you're racing that might be outside the championship," Gordon said. "And there was absolutely no reason to run into me."

Bowyer was still angry Friday about the Phoenix incident and didn't want to discuss Gordon.

"I don't want to talk about it. I really don't," he said as he walked from pit road to his team hauler.

Asked how long it would take for him to get past his anger, Bowyer said he didn't know, "It'll be a while." And when told he's not one to usually hold a grudge, he replied, "I'm usually not a guy that usually causes any trouble, either."

The only thing Gordon feels badly about is Logano getting collected in the accident. He said he spoke to Logano on the phone and "I can't say it went exactly very well" and he'd like to follow-up at the track.

Logano agreed the call did not go well.

"I reached out for an apology and I didn't get one, and I got hung up on," Logano said. "But he did text me, and I'm sure we'll meet up at some point. We're going to be able to go out and figure it out. We're big boys."

As for what's next, Gordon doesn't know. But he understands the attention on the incident with Bowyer, and the effect it might have on the season finale.

"I would tune in the following Sunday and see what happens," he said.

BOWYER AND GORDON STILL NOT SPEAKING
Las Vegas, Friday, November 30, 2012

Not even the party atmosphere in Las Vegas can cut the tension between Jeff Gordon and Clint Bowyer.

The two drivers haven't spoken since Gordon intentionally wrecked Bowyer at Phoenix on November 11, an incident that triggered a garage-area melee between the drivers' crews and earned Gordon a $100,000 fine from NASCAR.

Gordon said Thursday that the season-ending activities this week in Las Vegas have been "awkward" because he and Bowyer haven't socialized. Bowyer is popular among the other drivers and considered the life of the party.

"It's been awkward because I've always had a good relationship with him, we've always talked and had fun," Gordon said. "That's obviously not the case. I thought he might have gotten over it at least enough to look at me, but he won't even look at me, and when you are in this type of environment, that's going to be odd."

Bowyer, meanwhile, still doesn't want to discuss the incident. He and Gordon spoke in the NASCAR hauler at Phoenix, but haven't talked since.

Bowyer would not talk about it with reporters during the season finale at Homestead and on Thursday indicated he's not ready to resolve the issue with Gordon. He three times tried to change the subject, even once attempting to instead talk about nightclubs before finally growing exasperated.

"Good God," he said. "Is that my story I have to talk about?"

When told it was the story until it's resolved, Bowyer indicated he's not ready to resolve the issue with Gordon.

"I ain't resolving it," he said. "It probably ain't going to happen. It probably ain't going to get resolved this year. No more races."

Bowyer abruptly ended his media availability a few moments later, saying he was ready to go get changed out of his suit.

Bowyer still wasn't biting during a fan event at Planet Hollywood when he and Gordon's faces were superimposed on a pair of broken hearts as Taylor Swift's "We Are Never Ever Getting Back Together" played.

"Oh it ain't mended," he said. "Let's make fun of someone else."

But Bowyer was able to make fun of his now infamous run from pit road to the Phoenix garage, where his crew was fighting after the accident. The run was replayed Thursday at the "After the Lap" fan event in slow motion to the "Chariots of Fire" theme song.

Gordon said earlier Thursday he was unsure if he and Bowyer would get past this issue.

"Listen, I'm not here to make friends," he said. "I like his friendship. It can stay this way. But we have to race each other, I know what this all came about from and he might not agree and I'm sure we're going to disagree about a lot of things and we'll go race on next year and see what happens."

Gordon, a four-time champion, said he retaliated at Phoenix in a heat of the moment reaction to a grudge he'd been carrying for at least seven months. He'd been angry with Bowyer since Martinsville in April, when Bowyer played a role in costing Hendrick Motorsports its 200th victory.

The race had been dominated that day by Gordon and teammate Jimmie Johnson, and a late caution had set up a restart with the teammates lined up side-by-side at the front. Bowyer restarted in the second row, on new tires, and got a shove from behind from Ryan Newman. He dove to the inside of Gordon and Johnson, made contact, and all three wrecked.

Although Bowyer and Gordon spoke at the track that day, the two drivers had other on-track incidents between them over the season, including another run-in at Martinsville last month, but they had a conversation after that, too.

But something made Gordon snap at Phoenix after late contact between the two. When Gordon retaliated, he mathematically eliminated Bowyer from championship contention.

GORDON ADDED TO CHASE FIELD AMID CONTROVERSY
Joliet, Illinois, Friday, September 13, 2013

Jeff Gordon was added to the Chase for the Sprint Cup championship Friday when NASCAR chairman Brian France used his power to make an unprecedented expansion to the field after two separate investigations into radio chatter revealed numerous instances of race manipulation.

France determined Gordon did not have a fair chance to race his way into the 12-driver field last Saturday night at Richmond because of the actions of at least three organizations over the closing laps at Richmond.

The four-time NASCAR champion was bumped from eligibility by Joey Logano, who unknowingly received assistance from two Michael Waltrip Racing drivers trying to aid their teammate. Logano also picked up another track position when David Gilliland apparently moved aside when Gilliland's team tried to bargain with Penske Racing over the radio.

"Too many things altered the event and gave an unfair disadvantage to Jeff and his team," France said. "More than anything it's just the right thing to do. There were just too many things that went on Saturday night."

It was a stunning conclusion to a surreal week for NASCAR, which should have been celebrating Sunday's start of the Chase at Chicagoland Speedway.

Instead, the sanctioning body has been scrambling to uncover who did what and why since Clint Bowyer spun his car with seven laps remaining at Richmond as 10 drivers jockeyed for the five available spots in the Chase.

NASCAR acted quickly in disciplining MWR on Monday night, then learned Wednesday of a second apparent problem involving Penske and Front Row Motorsports, which appeared to ask for a deal if Gilliland moved over for Logano.

Logano did get by Gilliland, who then seemed to slow down by at least 1 mph, according to an Associated Press review of radio communications and data.

France said NASCAR could not determine there was ever a deal between Front Row and Penske, but that putting Gordon in the Chase and placing Penske and Front Row on probation for the rest of the season was necessary to protect the integrity of the series.

Gordon, the four-time champion, now joins Hendrick Motorsports teammates Jimmie Johnson, the five-time champion, Dale Earnhardt Jr. and Kasey Kahne in the Chase.

"It's been a roller coaster ride of emotions this week. Unprecedented set of circumstances," Gordon said. "I'm extremely happy for this. We're proud to be in it. An incredible set of opportunities now lie on our shoulders to show we belong in the Chase."

Gordon goes into the Chase as the 13th seed, 15 points behind leader Matt Kenseth.

Owner Rick Hendrick was pleased with the ruling.

"I applaud NASCAR for taking the time for a full review," he said in a statement. "We're extremely proud to have all four cars in the Chase for the second consecutive season. Jeff and the No. 24 team earned this spot."

Johnson was happy for his teammate but not thrilled to have an additional driver to race for the title.

"I believe there should be 12 cars. One in and one out should be the deal," he said.

Trading favors on and off the track is common in NASCAR, but the series had to investigate the Penske and Front Row bargaining allegation following the embarrassment of Michael Waltrip Racing's attempt to manipulate the out-come of the race to benefit

Martin Truex Jr. NASCAR on Monday punished the MWR organization for its shenanigans over the final seven laps and pulled Truex out of the Chase in favor of Ryan Newman.

Truex, in his first comments since he was knocked out of the Chase on Monday, said it's been a surreal week. An unwitting victim of his teammates' efforts to help him, he lost his Chase bid after driving the last two weeks with two broken bones in his wrist and a cast on his right arm.

"All I did the last two weeks was drive my heart out," he said Friday. "I went from feeling like I really climbed a mountain in that race at Richmond to going to be knocked out of the Chase."

Truex wasn't pleased with NASCAR's decision to add Gordon to the Chase.

"I'm not even sure what to say at this point. I'm kind of at a loss for words," Truex said. "How they make a spot for somebody they kick me out to make a spot for somebody and then they don't do the same for the other guys? It's just unfair and nothing I can do about it."

Truex is out as punishment for his teammates' working so hard to help him get in, and NASCAR will hold a mandatory team and driver meeting Saturday to clarify "the rules of the road" moving forward. France would not specify what won't be tolerated going forward.

"Obviously we drew a line with the penalties with Michael Waltrip Racing," France said. "We're going to make sure that we have the right rules going forward, so that the integrity of the competitive landscape of the events are not altered in a way or manipulated."

The entire mess began a mere seven laps from the finish Saturday night with Newman en route to a victory that would have given him the final spot in the Chase. MWR driver Clint Bowyer spun, bringing out a caution and setting in motion a chain of events that cost Newman the win and a Chase berth.

It also cost Gordon a Chase berth and put Truex and Logano into the final two spots.

It later became clear that Bowyer's spin was deliberate although NASCAR has said it can't prove that and that Bowyer and teammate Brian Vickers allowed Logano to gain late finishing positions to bump Gordon out of the Chase to aid Truex.

Among the penalties levied against MWR was a $300,000 fine and the indefinite suspension of general manager Ty Norris. Bowyer, Truex and Brian Vickers were docked 50 points each, and their crew chiefs were placed on probation through the end of the year.

Bowyer has denied the spin was deliberate. NASCAR could only prove one action radio communication between Norris and Vickers in which a confused Vickers was told to pit as the field went green with three laps to go.

Once NASCAR singled out that action, a Pandora's box was opened and the apparent bargaining between Penske and Front Row became dicey.

And Gordon's anger began to grow. Gordon said he felt that Bowyer also deserved to be punished for giving up late track position, just as Vickers did, and he called NASCAR's penalties "half right."

And now he's in the Chase with Bowyer but only after the second controversy.

RELATIONSHIP WITH BOWYER FOREVER DAMAGED
Charlotte, North Carolina, Wednesday, November 6, 2013

When NASCAR drivers gathered in Las Vegas last year to celebrate the end of the season, Jeff Gordon thought Clint Bowyer's rage toward him might have eased in the two weeks following an on-track spin and an off-track melee between their crews.

Bowyer, the life of every party, had no intention of including Gordon in the fun.

"I thought he might have gotten over it at least enough to look at me, but he won't even look at me, and when you are in this type of environment, that's going to be odd," Gordon said last November.

A full year removed from the Phoenix debacle, the relationship isn't much improved.

"It's affected our friendship, for sure," Gordon said. "I like Clint, he's a funny guy, a fun guy to hang out with. So we're not doing much hanging out these days. But also, I'm not there to make friends. So it's just racing as usual for me."

Gordon intentionally wrecked Bowyer in the closing laps of last November's race at Phoenix. On the surface, it appeared Gordon was retaliating for contact by Bowyer six laps earlier that cut one of Gordon's tires.

Furious over the damage, he spun Bowyer into the wall while creating an accident that also collected Joey Logano and effectively ended Bowyer's championship chances. An enraged Bowyer sprinted from his car into the garage, where crews for both drivers were fighting.

NASCAR fined Gordon $100,000 and docked him 25 points, but allowed the four-time champion to race in the season finale at Homestead, where he revealed that his anger with Bowyer dated back months. Bowyer first ran afoul of Gordon and the entire Hendrick Motorsports team on a late restart at Martinsville that caused an accident and cost Gordon and teammate Jimmie Johnson a shot at picking up the 200th win for the organization.

Gordon isn't sure the relationship with Bowyer, one of the most popular drivers in the garage, can ever be fully repaired.

"That was big, that was a major thing that happened between us and a heated exchange in the (NASCAR) hauler afterwards, too," Gordon said. "I don't think it will ever be quite like it was. We've spoken since and laughed about a few things, so I'm not saying we won't ever have a few beers together."

Bowyer to this day doesn't like talking about the Phoenix fracas with Gordon. Involved in his own controversy this year for intentionally spinning at Richmond in an effort to help teammate Martin Truex Jr. make the Chase for the Sprint Cup championship, he joked last week the one upside of the Richmond firestorm was that it blew over far quicker than the Phoenix incident.

"That (Richmond) was my own doing, but what happened at Phoenix lasted a whole other year," Bowyer said. "To put the magnitude of the situations, somehow (Richmond) went away in a month, and (Phoenix) lasted a whole year."

Beyond that, Bowyer didn't bite on discussing Phoenix any further.

The two drivers have done a good job of avoiding on-track controversy between each other this season.

"He hasn't run into me, that's been a positive," Gordon said. "He and I have always raced one another hard, but clean."

NO DISSRESPECT TO KEZ: Jimmie Johnson insists his crew chief meant to disrespect to defending NASCAR champion Brad

Keselowski when he called Matt Kenseth "a more formidable opponent" in their bid for a sixth title.

Chad Knaus made the reference following Sunday's dominating win at Texas, which put Johnson and the No. 48 team up by seven points over Kenseth headed to Phoenix this weekend. It's the same advantage Johnson held a year ago over Keselowski, who went on to win his first Sprint Cup title.

Keselowski won the championship in part because Johnson had a tire issue at Phoenix and a mechanical failure in the finale at Homestead.

Johnson downplayed Knaus' remark, and pointed out that Keselowski was going for his first title with a young crew chief in Paul Wolfe and a Penske Racing organization that had never before won a Sprint Cup championship.

"It wasn't any disrespect to the 2 team," Johnson said. "It was kind of based on experience. Paul, somewhat new, first championship battle. Brad, same thing."

The flipside is Kenseth, a 31-race winner and the 2003 series champion. Although crew chief Jason Ratcliff is in his first Sprint Cup title fight, Joe Gibbs Racing has won three championships since 2000.

"You look at the 20's situation ... Matt, not his first experience," Johnson said. "There's a little more experience in general. That's what ultimately (Knaus) was trying to say."

CANADIAN ATHLETE OF THE YEAR: It was a breakthrough season in IndyCar for James Hinchcliffe, who grabbed his first career victory in the season-opener at St. Petersburg and added wins at Brazil and Iowa before the year was over.

It was enough to earn Hinchcliffe a nomination for 2013 Canadian Athlete of the Year Award. The award is selected by voters on sportsnet.ca.

"It's an honor to receive a nomination and I'm simply proud to be on the list in amongst so many outstanding Canadians," Hinchcliffe said. "We can all be super proud of our accomplishments as athletes this year and it shows the strength and determination of Canadians to succeed in competitive environments. Even better, it's a fan vote and in my opinion that's all the matters as they're the people who matter."

Voting runs online through November 15.

Hinchcliffe is one of 16 nominees and is up against the likes of three-time world champion figure skater Patrick Chan, golfer Graham DeLaet, world champion bobsledder Kaillie Humphries, mixed martial artist Georges St-Pierre, two-time reigning Winter X Games champion snowboarder Mark McMorris and curler Rachel Homan.

DOUBLE STANDARDS FOR KESELOWSKI?
Charlotte, North Carolina, Monday, November 3, 2014

In the closing laps at Martinsville Speedway, Jeff Gordon could see Dale Earnhardt Jr. ahead of him with enough time to formulate a plan on how to handle his teammate if Gordon could catch him.

Earnhardt had been eliminated from the Chase for the Sprint Cup championship field one week earlier and was racing only for a trophy. Gordon, still eligible to win the title, wanted to win last week to grab the automatic berth into the final round of NASCAR's playoffs.

Jeff Gordon is in the middle of a fight after the NASCAR Sprint Cup Series auto race at Texas Motor Speedway. The crews of Gordon and Brad Keselowski fought after the race, November 2, 2014. (AP Photo/Matthew Bishop)

So what would have happened?

"I would have moved him for sure. There's no doubt in my mind," Gordon said after finishing second to Earnhardt at Martinsville. "Everybody who is out there racing has to weigh risk versus reward. For me, to win this race, it's worth taking a lot of risk, even if you upset your teammate.

"I think everybody out there that's not in the Chase understands that if that guy can win that race and put himself in Homestead for the championship, you can pretty much guarantee that you're going to get the bumper or get slammed or something."

Well, Gordon got slammed on Sunday at Texas Motor Speedway and he didn't like it one bit. He confronted Brad Keselowski on pit road following the race, and an exchange of words escalated quickly - with an assist from Kevin Harvick - into a full-blown melee between the crews.

Both champions were left bloodied - Gordon's lip and Keselowski spitting blood after taking a shot to the cheek - even though neither driver appeared to throw a punch or get close enough to each other to actually fight.

But for the second time in four races, Keselowski was attacked in a post-race fracas because his aggressive driving upset someone. It happened at Charlotte last month when Denny Hamlin had to be restrained from going after him, then Matt Kenseth jumped him from behind before he was quickly pulled away.

This time, Gordon was primed for a smack-down. He called his shot on his team radio when he said he was going to beat up Keselowski, who on a restart during an overtime two-lap sprint to the finish tried to wedge his car in between Gordon and teammate Jimmie Johnson to grab the lead.

There were two laps left at the time and Keselowski, in a hole in the Chase standings, needed that win to grab one of the four spots in the November 16 championship finale at Homestead-Miami Speedway. He saw a gap and went for it, just as any driver with his season on the line should have done. Gordon himself said just seven days earlier everyone should expect Chase drivers to be aggressive.

The problem was that Keselowski and Gordon made contact, causing Gordon to spin after his tire went flat. Racing for a win and a spot at Homestead moments earlier, he wound up finishing 29th and is fourth in the eight-driver Chase field.

It's understandable that Gordon was angry. But it's unfair to hold Keselowski to a different standard, even if his body of work has drawn the ire of the majority of the garage.

Keselowski had as much on the line as Gordon, and it was a go-for-broke, risk versus reward moment where Keselowski let it all hang out.

"Brad Keselowski is a champion who competes to win in every race, which is what I expect of him," team owner Roger Penske said in a statement Monday. "While the actions by others following the race in Texas were unfortunate, Brad has my 100 percent support as we now move on to Phoenix for the next stage of the NASCAR championship."

The late Formula One champion Ayrton Senna said repeatedly throughout his career that drivers always compete to win. "If you no longer go for a gap that exists, you are no longer a racing driver because we are competing, we are competing to win," he said in 1990.

Senna and so many other greats raced under those standards. Gordon himself said just a week ago that aggression is warranted at this stage of the season. Why is not OK for Keselowski to do the same?

Some other elements of the Sunday night fight that should be addressed:

HARVICK THE PUPPET MASTER: The pit road fight might never have happened had Harvick not rushed in from behind the scrum and shoved Keselowski in the back toward the tempest. Fists were flying seconds later, and Harvick backed his way out and returned to a bystander role.

Harvick is the quintessential Machiavellian character in NASCAR. He's always loved stirring the pot and pulling the strings from behind the curtain. It's part of his game, and climbing into the head of his competitors gives Harvick an edge.

He knew exactly what he was doing with that shove: Also in a hole in the Chase, Harvick benefits from all the other title contenders being locked into a drama that disrupts their focus as they head this week to Phoenix.

Harvick has won three of the last four races at Phoenix and should be the favorite Sunday. But Gordon was in another league when Hendrick Motorsports tested at Phoenix last month, and Keselowski has already proved once in this Chase (at Talladega) that he can produce in must-win races.

Unless NASCAR takes issue with Harvick's role as instigator in this brawl, he walks away scot-free as two of his top rivals find themselves in an uncomfortable spotlight.

CREW MEMBERS: Harvick contends he was simply telling Keselowski to handle his business after the on-track incident with Gordon, and there's been fan backlash that Keselowski was hiding behind his crew members when Gordon approached.

The reality is, Gordon and Keselowski were never getting close to each other to have a reasonable discussion or even a fight. There's always a cavalry of adrenaline-fueled crew members who jump into these post-race confrontations, and Sunday night's was a Hendrick Motorsports schoolyard brawl. Punches were thrown from every direction and multiple video angles show Keselowski took at least one to the face and one to the back of the head.

The most egregious action came from a member of Kasey Kahne's crew who rushed in from behind and threw haymakers in defense of Hendrick driver Gordon, who at one time grabbed at Keselowski's fire suit but was quickly pulled away.

NASCAR is reviewing the entire matter, and Hendrick Motorsports said Monday it was also doing an internal review. Kenseth dodged a penalty after Charlotte because he didn't throw a punch at Keselowski, and NASCAR doesn't have much of a reason to punish Gordon or Keselowski.

But the goon like behavior from the crews must sternly be addressed - and halted. The drivers started this on the track and had the right to end it off of it without the assistance of others.

Chapter 7

FINAL HURRAH

NASCAR driver Jeff Gordon (24) crosses the finish line to win the Sprint Cup Series auto race at Kansas Speedway in Kansas City, Kansas, May 10, 2014. (AP Photo/Orlin Wagner)

FIFTH TITLE?
Daytona Beach, Florida, Thursday, February 13, 2014

Jeff Gordon is prepared to retire if he can win a fifth NASCAR championship.

The 42-year-old Gordon won championships in 1995, 1997, 1998 and 2001. He won all of them when NASCAR's top series ran under the Winston Cup banner.

He wants to win a Sprint Cup championship. With a family at home, a fifth title could convince him to call it quits.

"If that happened, that would be all the reasons I need to say, this is it. I'm done," Gordon says. "Go out on a high note."

Gordon said recently he was "jokingly serious" about retiring after another championship.

At Daytona, he insisted he was serious.

"I go home and I look at my trophy room. I see four trophies, championship trophies," he said Thursday at Daytona 500 media day. "But they say Winston Cup on them. You can name me a four-time Sprint Cup champion for technical reasons all you want, but to me, I'm still not. I want that before my career's over."

He would love to make a push in the No. 24 in the revamped Chase for the Sprint Cup championship.

Gordon was added to the Chase last season when NASCAR chairman Brian France used his power to make an unprecedented expansion to the field after two separate investigations into radio chatter revealed numerous instances of race manipulation at Richmond.

France determined Gordon did not have a fair chance to race his way into the 12-driver field because of the actions of at least three organizations over the closing laps.

Gordon was sixth last season in the standings, his best finish since he was third in 2009.

He has 88 Cup victories, third on the career Cup list, and has had only two winless seasons since 1993.

"I've put in 20-plus great years," he said "I do this now because I love it, because I like being competitive, and because I want another championship. I want to get a Sprint Cup championship."

GORDON PULLS AWAY LATE FOR KANSAS WIN
Kansas City, Kansas, Sunday, May 11, 2014

At any age, Jeff Gordon sure knows how to win.

Nearly two decades after he burst onto the scene with his first victory, Gordon keeps taking checkered flags, storming to the lead in the final laps at Kansas Speedway on Saturday night for his first victory of the season and 89th overall in NASCAR's top series.

The 42-year-old Gordon held off a hard-charging Kevin Harvick on the final lap to move into the Chase for the Sprint Cup championship field.

Gordon won for the first time since October at Martinsville and became the ninth driver to win in the first 11 races this season. He entered the race with the points lead, but exclaimed a weight was lifted off his shoulders as he crossed the finish line for his third Kansas victory.

"I'm just so proud of (the 24 team). They have been giving me the best race cars all year long," Gordon said. "I have been having so much fun. I'm going to be 43 this year and I feel like I'm 25 again. That is the way they make me feel."

Kasey Kahne was third, followed by Joey Logano and Dale Earnhardt Jr.

Danica Patrick was seventh for her best career Cup finish.

Gordon built his points lead on the strength of four top-fives and seven top-10s in the first 10 races - including second-place finishes at Texas and Richmond - but he knew how much one win would ease pressure on his Hendrick Motorsports team.

He got it under the lights at Kansas.

"This is so sweet," he said. "What a huge weight lifted off this team's shoulders. We needed to get to Victory Lane."

Gordon is celebrating the 20th anniversary of his first career Cup victory at Charlotte Motor Speedway in the prestigious Coca-Cola 600. He will go for his fourth Coca-Cola 600 victory May 25.

At Daytona this year, Gordon insisted he was serious about considering retirement with a fifth championship. He looks every bit a title contender - but said he feels like he could race until 50 if his cars are this stout.

"The whole retirement thing I think is thrown out too much," he said. "I know I'm somewhat to blame for that."

After the start of the race was delayed 35 minutes by rain, the first Sprint Cup night race at Kansas soon left drivers in the dark after the lights went out on the backstretch. NASCAR polled drivers if they wanted to continue and they were good to go, with Kurt Busch and Carl Edwards among the many who said the track was bright enough to race.

Harvick led the final 36 laps in his October win and led the first 41 on Saturday before briefly falling into the middle of the pack. Harvick worked his way to the front in the No. 4 Chevrolet and opened a commanding lead over Gordon and Logano. He led a race-high 119 laps in the 400-mile race - small consolation once Gordon grabbed the lead with eight to go.

With two wins already, Harvick has been a force in his first season at Stewart-Haas Racing, but his dominant Chevrolet ran out of gas on his last pit stop and lost time that he couldn't recover.

"I should have been paying attention to my pit road lights and should have got off pit road better," he said. "I made a mistake at the end and it cost us a chance to stay out in front of the 24."

Patrick had her best run of the season, spending most of the race nestled inside the top 10, and brought a needed jolt of electricity when she passed teammate Tony Stewart and Earnhardt to move into third with 95 laps left.

Patrick hadn't finished better this season than 14th at Fontana and her lone top-10 in the Cup series was an eighth-place finish in the 2013 Daytona 500.

She was shuffled back on a restart, costing her a top five.

Patrick beamed in the garage after the kind of finish she'd been striving for since her dazzling performance at Daytona more than a year ago.

Crew chief Tony Gibson told her, "Chicks rule, huh?"

"I know that we haven't had the best of times, but we work hard for it," Patrick said. "This is the kind of stuff that materializes in wins. We've just got to keep hanging around and doing what we're doing. I'm just proud of everyone for working really hard and believing in me."

Sara Christian's fifth-place finish in a 1949 race remains the best for a female driver in NASCAR's top series.

Jamie McMurray and David Gilliland both had their cars erupt in flames in separate accidents. Gilliland was slow to exit his No. 38 Ford and gingerly walked away from the smoldering wreckage. He was checked out and released from the infield care center.

"It was the hardest hit I've had in a long time," he said.

McMurray had a solid run derailed when he smacked the wall and the back of his No. 1 Chevrolet caught fire.

"I heard a small pop, and then just lost all the steering and got into the fence," he said.

BACK SPASMS
Concord, North Carolina, Saturday, May 24, 2014

Sprint Cup points leader Jeff Gordon cut short his practice because of back spasms and the No. 24 team has Regan Smith on standby should the four-time champion not be able to run the Coca-Cola 600 on Sunday night.

Gordon went just 11 laps Saturday before he told his crew he couldn't continue. He left out of a side door of his hauler and was escorted out of the track to get treatment. Crew chief Alan Gustafson said the team would not run the car in the final practice session and instead will get it ready for Sunday's race.

"I've had some spasms in the past, but this one, it was a little bit different," said the 42-year-old Gordon. "And so I just want to really be cautious and take care of it. It doesn't do me any good to be in the car right now."

Gustafson said the plan was for Gordon to start the longest event in NASCAR. Should the pain be too much, then Smith would take over the Hendrick Motorsports car.

Gustafson said Gordon felt back pain after qualifying Thursday night and had hoped things would improve before Saturday's practice sessions. But "after the first run, we talked about it and it was pretty detrimental to him physically to continue," Gustafson said.

Gordon said on Twitter he planned to rest and "be ready for 600 miles 2moro."

The four-time series champion is having one of the steadiest starts of his career with eight top-10 finishes in the first 11 races. Gordon moved into the points lead following a second-place finish at Texas Motor Speedway in early April and he's stayed out front ever since. He cemented his place in the Sprint Cup's championship Chase two weeks ago with a victory at Kansas Speedway.

Gordon will start 27th and hope his back holds out for 400 laps around the 1.5-mile race track.

"Luckily, we had a good 11 laps there and we've got our teammates and information that we're going to be able to gather from them," Gordon said. "It's all coming together very fast right now."

Gordon has had back spasms in the past and even considered retiring because of the severe pain. Regular treatment has kept the pain mostly in check and Gustafson hopes that will be the case again for Sunday.

Doctors "will get him in the best condition he can and get him ready to run tomorrow," Gustafson said.

This week's race marks the 20th anniversary of Gordon's first Sprint Cup victory. His crew chief then, Ray Evernham, said Gordon is much tougher than some believe and has raced through illness and pain before.

"We won the Southern 500 (at Darlington) when he started throwing up halfway" through the race, said Evernham, currently working for Hendrick Motorsports.

Evernham said Gordon believes his car is ready and is being smart by not hurting himself further by practicing.

"He'll do everything he needs to do to get to feeling good and I know him and tomorrow night in that car, he may need some help getting out of it, but when he's in it, he's going to be at 100 percent," Evernham said.

GORDON COULD RETIRE OVER BACK WOES
Dover, Delaware, Friday, May 30, 2014

Four-time NASCAR champion Jeff Gordon said Friday he will have to retire if he continues to suffer the same, excruciating back pain that he did before last weekend's Coca-Cola 600.

The 42-year-old Gordon is in no hurry to slow down. But he said he hopes he has found some solutions to the back woes that nearly forced him out of NASCAR's longest race. Gordon cut short his practice runs last week because of back spasms and there was some concern whether or not he would be able to race.

Regan Smith was on standby and Gordon needed treatment after the practice session. But he wound up in his familiar seat behind the wheel of the No. 24 and finished seventh, his ninth top-10 finish in 12 races this season.

Gordon knows consistent, shooting pain like he suffered at Charlotte Motor Speedway could drive him toward an early retirement.

"I can tell you, if that happens many more times, I won't have a choice," Gordon said Friday at Dover Motor Speedway.

Gordon had soreness Monday and Tuesday, though that didn't deviate too much from how he would feel after driving 600 grueling miles. He said his back is not at 100 percent, and probably never will be behind the wheel.

At Daytona this year, Gordon insisted he was serious about considering retirement should he win a fifth championship. He looks every bit a title contender - he has a win and holds the points lead - and gutting out Charlotte proved to his Hendrick Motorsports team "it's going to take a lot to get us down."

Gordon suffered serious issues years ago in his back, specifically his lower spine, and needed anti-inflammatory medication and workouts with a trainer to return to full strength. He drove in pain during a winless 2008 season and briefly contemplated retirement.

For all his back woes, Gordon said he never felt the stabbing pain there like he did last weekend.

Gordon said he'll make adjustments to his race weekend routine to keep his back loose to withstand hours crunched in a stock car. He needs to stay active and not sit during lengthy breaks in practice and qualifying. Gordon sat more than three hours last week between practice and qualifying, a gap that left he believed led his creaky back to a breakdown.

"Once that happened, there was nothing that was going to fix it until I had those injections on Saturday," he said.

Gordon has no standby driver at Dover. He felt fine on Friday. But once inside the No. 24, all bets are off.

"It's just something I continue to learn and push through," he said. "It's no big deal."

CONTENT WITH 2ND PLACE FINISH AT SONOMA
Sonoma, California, Monday, June 23, 2014

There's no better driver at Sonoma Raceway than Jeff Gordon, and for more than a decade he was head of the class on road courses.

He won five times at Sonoma, and grabbed another four wins at Watkins Glen. But Gordon's last win on a road course was 2006. The rest of the field has caught up and Gordon is no longer considered unbeatable.

Yet there he was on Sunday, charging through the field from the 15th position - he was the highest qualifying Hendrick Motorsports driver - to give himself a shot at a sixth Sonoma victory. But he made one small error while chasing down Carl Edwards, so it took him longer to get to the leader than expected.

When he finally made it to Edwards' bumper in the final turn of the 10-turn course, Gordon declined to move Edwards out of his way. The four-time champion let Edwards go, and Edwards sailed off to his first career road course victory.

Gordon settled for second, his third runner-up finish this season.

"It's not worth wrecking the guy because, hey, if you're racing the guy and you get a couple runs on him, he blocks you here and he blocks you there and you're faster, then you might not give an inch," Gordon said. "You might go in there and you might use the bumper. But I really had just caught him."

So Gordon felt his best bet was to try to force Edwards into making a mistake that Gordon would seize. Edwards held it together and shook Gordon loose.

During the Victory Lane celebration, Gordon came by to congratulate the winner. The move touched Edwards.

"I'm a fan of this sport and I grew up watching Jeff Gordon go through thoses's and watching how he drove his car," Edwards said. "So to be able to hold him off like that means a lot. I'm glad there wasn't one or two more laps in the race because I don't know if it would have worked out that way, but it definitely meant a lot to have Jeff Gordon in my mirror."

At almost 43 years old, those are sentiments Gordon is hearing more frequently as he's become the elder statesman of the Sprint Cup Series.

Mark Martin has called it a career, Jeff Burton is transitioning into a television job and Bobby Labonte no longer has a ride. Gordon's contemporaries are climbing out of their race cars, but at the start of his third decade in NASCAR, Gordon is still getting it done.

"I'm starting to hear that a lot more, where somebody was born when I won my first championship or was watching me as a kid," Gordon said. "I love racing here. I love being competitive and leading the points and having a shot at winning races, at 22 years into my Cup career. We're having fun."

He should be: With 10 races remaining to set the Chase for the Sprint Cup championship field, Gordon has a 20-point lead over teammate Jimmie Johnson in the points standings. He has the one win needed to lock him into the 16-driver Chase field. Toss out an accident-induced 39th-place finish at Talladega and Gordon hasn't finished lower than 15th this year.

Gordon has failed to finish in the top-10 just four times in 16 races this season.

Yes, winning has a greater emphasis this season. But consistency still matters down the stretch.

Gordon still faces persistent questions about retirement. Part of that is driven by age and the fact that the father of two young children has the luxury to choose when he wants to get off the road and become a family man. And part of that is driven by an aching back that has bothered him for years.

It flared up again in May before the Coca-Cola 600, and Gordon is receiving regular treatment. He insists he feels fine, though, and the flight from North Carolina to San Francisco was more stressful on his back than the three-plus hours in a race car.

Sure, there's going to come a day when Gordon decides he's done with racing. But based on his current performance, it's not anytime soon.

"It's certainly the most consistent, greatest cars that I've had going week in and week out," he said. "To have cars that are capable of either winning or running up front, I'm very confident in what I'm getting behind the wheel of every weekend. The cars are just really, really good, and that's making a lot of fun for me."

'JEFF GORDON DAY' AT INDY FOR RECORD 5TH TIME
Indianapolis, Sunday, July 27, 2014

With a tinge of gray hair at his temples, his hat on backward and his two young children by his side, Jeff Gordon celebrated as if he was 23 years old again.

Gordon won a NASCAR-record fifth Brickyard 400 on Sunday, eight days before his 43rd birthday and on the weekend Indianapolis Motor Speedway celebrated the 20th anniversary of his first Brickyard victory.

Gordon's first win came before the celebratory kissing of the Yard of Bricks was en vogue, before he became a household name, while Sprint Cup Series rookies Kyle Larson and Austin Dillon were still in diapers. Now a family man with an aching back, Gordon used Sunday to show he's still at the top of his game.

"If you can do it here, you can do it anywhere," said Gordon, who has led the Sprint Cup Series standings for 13 of the last 14 weeks. "It's certainly going to be a huge confidence boost for this team. We recognize the significance of this.

"We saw we were points leaders, we won at Kansas, but I don't know if we believed we were capable of winning this championship this year. We do now."

Jeff Gordon celebrates after winning the NASCAR Brickyard 400 auto race at Indianapolis Motor Speedway, July 27, 2014. (AP Photo/AJ Mast)

To prove it to himself, to his Hendrick Motorsports team and to his ardent fan base, Gordon needed a vintage close to Sunday's race.

Hendrick teammate Kasey Kahne led a race-high 70 laps and seemed only to be racing against his gas tank when a late caution put the race back into Gordon's hands. He'd have one shot at passing Kahne, on a dreaded restart, and nobody was sure if ol' "Four-Time" had it in him.

Restarts are his Achilles heel, and he's struggled with them for several years. And Kahne, who is winless on the season, desperately needed the victory to grab a berth in the Chase for the Sprint Cup championship field.

"The restart is going to be the race, really," Gordon's crew chief, Alan Gustafson, conceded in a television interview moments before the field went green with 17 laps remaining.

Kahne picked the lower, inside lane for the restart, and Gordon found himself on the outside and exactly where he wanted to be. Gordon tried to set a quick pace as they headed to the flag, and Kahne tried to slow it down in the restart zone.

Gordon shifted into fourth gear and surged past Kahne on the outside, and Gordon kicked it into cruise control as he sailed away for the win.

"I think we both knew that was for the win," Gordon said of Kahne. "Out of nowhere, I have the restart of my life at the most important moment that you could ask for in a race, in a season, at a race like this. That was just awesome."

The win came on the 20th anniversary celebration of Gordon's win in the inaugural Brickyard 400, and on "Jeff Gordon Day" as declared by the Mayor of Indianapolis. The win moved Gordon into a tie with Michael Schumacher, whose five Formula One victories at Indy had been the gold standard.

"I told him this morning that this was his day," said team owner Rick Hendrick.

Kahne plummeted to fifth after the restart, then ran out of gas on the final lap and had to nurse his car home to a sixth-place finish. He said he erred in picking the inside line for the restart.

"I should have chosen the top (lane), obviously," he said. "I pretty much let Jeff control that last restart. I thought I made the right decision."

Hendrick said he had no favorite in that situation, and hoped only that Gordon and Kahne did not wreck each other.

"I know Kasey, he needed a win, and he ran awful good today," Hendrick said. "But Jeff had the dominant car, so it all worked out."

Kyle Busch finished second, 2.325 seconds behind Gordon, and was followed by Joe Gibbs Racing teammates Denny Hamlin and Matt Kenseth. After the race, NASCAR said Hamlin's car had failed post-race inspection and the parts in question would be taken to North Carolina for another look.

Joey Logano was fifth in the highest-finishing car from Team Penske, which brought Juan Pablo Montoya to the race in an effort to get the win. Roger Penske has won a record 15 Indianapolis 500s, but is winless in the Brickyard. Montoya was never a factor and finished 23rd.

Larson, who grew up a Gordon fan, finished seventh and likened Gordon's win on Sunday to Dale Earnhardt Jr.'s season-opening win in the Daytona 500.

"To see Jeff Gordon win is pretty special - it's kind of like Junior winning the 500 this year," Larson said.

Kevin Harvick, the polesitter and the driver with the car most everyone thought would be tough to beat, was eighth and followed by Earnhardt and rookie Austin Dillon.

Carl Edwards finished 15th hours after Roush-Fenway Racing finally confirmed he was leaving the team at the end of the season.

In addition to his 1994 victory, Gordon also won at the track in 1998, 2001 and 2004.

He has 90 Cup wins, third on the career list.

He said it took extreme focus over the final 10 laps not to prematurely celebrate and cough away the win. It meant tuning out the crowd, which was on its feet and cheering him to the finish.

"I was trying not to let it get to me and not think about it too much," he said. "And yet you can't help it. It's such a big place and such an important victory and a crucial moment in the season and the championship, and those emotions take over.

"This one is for all those fans throughout the years and all weekend long - they're saying 'We believe you can get (championship) number five.' We got (Brickyard) No. 5!"

GORDON EYES 5TH TITLE AFTER BRICKYARD WIN
Indianapolis, Sunday, July 28, 2014

Long before Jimmie Johnson arrived on the NASCAR scene, Jeff Gordon was the fastest thing on wheels.

He was the "Wonder Boy" who racked up wins at a record place. He brought the southern sport to Madison Avenue and became such a household name that even rapper Nelly name-dropped Gordon in a song.

Gordon won all the big races, collected four championships in seven years and had 58 victories before his 30th birthday.

Then his pace began to slow, the rest of the field caught up to him and Johnson moved into the Hendrick Motorsports shop as the new kid on the block. Gordon hasn't won a title since, while Johnson has won five.

Now, 13 years after Gordon launched "The Drive for 5," Gordon is on track to collect that elusive fifth title.

The Sprint Cup points leader won Sunday's Brickyard 400, a race that often gives a preview of the championship. Nine times in 21 years, the winner at Indianapolis Motor Speedway went on to hoist the Cup at the end of the year.

"If you can do it here, you can do it anywhere," Gordon said after his NASCAR-record fifth win at Indy.

Gordon, a week shy of his 43rd birthday and often fighting an aching back, won on the 20th anniversary celebration of his first Brickyard victory. It came on the day the Mayor of Indianapolis proclaimed "Jeff Gordon Day" and showed Gordon is trying to make 2014 his year.

Although he talked in January of retirement considerations, Gordon is reinvigorated and deeply committed to winning a title with his No. 24 team.

"You feel like you've kind of won all that you could win, you've won four championships, then a guy like Jimmie Johnson comes along and starts dominating, you kind of lose the motivation," Gordon said.

But he is inspired by the work ethic and dedication of crew chief Alan Gustafson, and fears being "the weak link" of the race team. He also is motivated to share his success with wife, Ingrid, and their two young children. Gordon married Ingrid in 2006 and the couple quickly added a boy and a girl to the family.

"It's pushed me to give more, do more, work harder," he said. "Ingrid has never experienced a championship. I told her 'Hey, I know you want to know what it's like to win a championship. Well, there's a big commitment that it takes.' She's like 'Whatever it takes.'

"That's the kind of year that we're having. We're just putting everything we possibly can into it."

It's going take everything Gordon has to win this Chase for the Sprint Cup championship, the first under a winner-take-all, elimination round format.

A model of consistency all season long with 14 top-10 finishes in 20 races, the slate will be wiped clean come September. Gordon will have to be aggressive and out front to make it through the three elimination rounds. If he is one of the four drivers to advance all the way to the Homestead finale, the title will go to the best driver in the fastest car on one day only.

That could be Gordon, if he drives anything like he did at Indy.

Although he's struggled with restarts for several years, and did most of Sunday, he finally nailed one when he needed it most.

A late caution gave him one shot at taking the lead away from teammate Kasey Kahne, and he figured a perfect strategy as they headed toward the green flag. Kahne had given Gordon the outside lane, and he knew if he was alongside Kahne in the corner, he'd be able to hold him down and loosen Kahne's car.

"I treated him like a competitor at that point, he might not have liked it," Gordon said. "When it comes down to the end of a race, we're here to win."

The victory was the 90th of Gordon's career, and he's just the third driver to hit that mark. Although it was once believed he might chase Richard Petty's record of 200 wins, David Pearson's 105 is suddenly in reach depending on how long Gordon wants to stay in his Chevrolet.

Pearson's total is a long way away for Gordon, but the championship is suddenly very near. His win in May at Kansas was motivating for driver and crew, but the win at Indy on Sunday convinced them all the title is a very real possibility.

"It's certainly a huge confidence boost for this team. We recognize the significance of this," he said. "I don't know if we believed we were capable of winning this championship this year, truly believed it. We do now."

NASCAR WINNER WITH JEFF AND JUNIOR ON TOP
Charlotte, North Carolina, Monday, August 4, 2014

It was Jeff Gordon's championship to lose just a week ago after his record fifth win at the Brickyard. Then Dale Earnhardt Jr. completed a season sweep at Pocono and now he's the guy to beat.

Jeff and Junior, two of NASCAR's biggest stars heating up during this lazy summer stretch of racing. NASCAR really couldn't ask for anything more.

Well, it wouldn't hurt if Tony Stewart threw his hat into the ring, too. As of Tuesday, it will be one year since the broken leg that ended his season, and Stewart has now gone 14 months without a victory. He is on the outside looking in on the Chase for the Sprint Cup championship field.

Stewart is one of the very few drivers who move the needle for NASCAR, and he has just five races remaining to grab a win he desperately needs to make him automatically eligible to race for the championship. For now, the only noise Smoke is making on the track is his constant sniping against blocking (do as he says, not as he does), but it might be time for him to block his way into Victory Lane.

That would give NASCAR the trifecta for its highly anticipated Chase, which for the first time will feature elimination rounds and a winner-take-all finale. Picture the glee on Brian France's face in Phoenix if it's some combination of Junior and Jeff, Smoke and Jimmie Johnson, Brad Keselowski, Kyle Busch and Kevin Harvick all jockeying to make the Final Four showdown at Homestead.

Maybe Stewart makes it, maybe he doesn't - and really, he needs to be in the Chase because the intensity is always higher when Smoke is involved - but that's just another element of this win-win time for NASCAR.

The powers that be can't ask for anything more than the 24 and 88 flexing their muscles right now, when neither team has anything to lose. They are playing with house money, having fun seeing what they are made of before the 10-race Chase.

For Gordon, the points leader for 14 of the last 15 weeks, it's about building the confidence of his team and making them believe a championship is possible. There was no doubt after the Brickyard victory, and he followed it by leading a race-high 63 laps Sunday at Pocono before finishing sixth.

The win went to Earnhardt, who used crew chief Steve Letarte's strategy to complete the Pocono sweep. It was his third win of the season - the same amount of victories Earnhardt earned all of 2006 through 2013 - and came just four days after Hendrick Motorsports announced Letarte's replacement for 2014.

It showed the 88 team isn't letting up, and Letarte is determined to guide Earnhardt to his first championship before he turns him over to Greg Ives at the end of the season.

Both will have to contend with Hendrick teammate Johnson, who may or may not be playing possum. He doesn't have a top-10 finish since the last week of June, but it's not unusual for Johnson, much like a swimmer, to taper off before turning it up several notches when everything is on the line.

Then there's Harvick, who seems to be up front and in contention every week, and Team Penske's Keselowski and Joey Logano. They've got a combined seven wins and eight poles between them, and all three are locked into the Chase and looking ahead to September.

But there are many drivers who don't have that luxury just yet, including Matt Kenseth, who fell just short of winning the title last season.

He's winless so far this year, and like his Joe Gibbs Racing teammates Kyle Busch and Denny Hamlin, not at the same performance level they were last season. While Kenseth should get in on points - he's fourth in the standings with five weeks to go - no one can take anything for granted.

Same goes for Clint Bowyer (ninth in points), Greg Biffle (13th) and Kasey Kahne (14th). They are all perennial Chase qualifiers, but could all be bumped if some longshots - see: Aric Almirola at Daytona - start winning some races. A coveted Chase spot could vanish if road course ringer Marcos Ambrose makes it to Victory Lane at Watkins Glen on Sunday.

NASCAR also could see hotshot rookies Kyle Larson, a success story from its diversity program, and Austin Dillon, the grandson of team owner Richard Childress, sneak their way into the Chase. Both are currently ranked inside the top 16 in the standings, and should there not be 16 race winners, they've got a shot at making the final cut.

The story lines are changing every week, and in these dog days of summer, a time when nothing used to matter in NASCAR, everything is going right.

FIRST WIN AT MICHIGAN SINCE 2001
Brooklyn, Michigan, Sunday, August 17, 2014

It had been 13 years since Jeff Gordon's last victory at Michigan - which came during the same season as his most recent championship on NASCAR's top series.

One of those droughts is finally over. Can the 43-year-old driver end the other as well?

"Certainly things are going well - there's no doubt about that," Gordon said. "I'm as shocked as anybody else."

Gordon raced to his third Sprint Cup victory of the year, holding off Kevin Harvick on Sunday for his first win at Michigan International Speedway since 2001.

Gordon broke the track qualifying record Friday when he took the pole at 206.558 mph. He followed that up with his third Cup victory at MIS - and took over the points lead from Hendrick Motorsports teammate Dale Earnhardt Jr.

After a series of cautions, Gordon came off the final restart well and led with 16 laps remaining. He fought off a challenge from Joey Logano and maintained a comfortable margin over Harvick, winning the 400-mile race by 1.412 seconds in his No. 24 Chevrolet.

"Joey, as we rolled up to some of the restarts - not that last one, but some of the other ones - as guys were starting to sort of anticipate it, he was slowing down, and when he slowed down, everybody got bottled up, and then he'd take off," Gordon said. "That last one, I thought he had a good start, but I had a good one, too."

Harvick was second, followed by Logano, Paul Menard and Earnhardt.

Gordon completed a sweep at MIS for Hendrick. Jimmie Johnson won the June race on the two-mile oval.

"I think all of our teams are running well, but this is a big, big win," owner Rick Hendrick said. "It's great to see Jeff so happy. He's like a little kid again, so I think it's going to be really, really important for the momentum he's carrying right now into the Chase."

Logano was second to Gordon in qualifying. He led 86 laps and Gordon was in front for 68.

"We can win a championship. I really feel we can do that. That's the message I want to put out there," Logano said. "We've got to find a little bit more speed to keep up with one car today - 24 car was the best, only because he was good on the long run. We weren't as good on the long run.

Jeff Gordon celebrates his victory with a burnout after the NASCAR Sprint Cup Series Pure Michigan 400 auto race at Michigan International Speedway, August 17, 2014. (AP Photo/Bob Brodbeck)

There were eight cautions, including a fairly early one when Danica Patrick's car spun and Justin Allgaier crashed into her. Nine cars were caught up in that incident, including Matt Kenseth's No. 20 Toyota.

Kenseth never really recovered, finishing 38th.

Brad Keselowski rubbed against the wall with about 32 laps remaining and finished eighth, remaining winless at this track in his home state. Johnson overcame some problems of his own to finish ninth, his first top-10 showing in six races.

Jeff Burton was 37th after replacing Tony Stewart in the No. 14 car. Stewart skipped his second straight Cup race after he struck and killed a driver at a dirt-track race in New York last weekend.

Hendrick and Stewart-Haas Racing are alliance teams. Hendrick said he hasn't talked to Stewart, but he's been in touch with Eddie Jarvis, Stewart's longtime business manager.

"I think they're making the best of the situation that they're in," Hendrick said. "Tony's got a lot of good folks around him."

Gordon won for the 91st time on the Cup circuit, and this is his first three-win season since 2011. He took over the lead in the standings by three points over Earnhardt.

Gordon also won this season at Kansas and Indianapolis.

"As a driver, especially somebody that's been getting beat up over the years about restarts, it's pretty nice to have the last two wins come down to restarts."

Assuming they attempt to qualify for the final three races of the regular-season, the 12 drivers with victories this season have all wrapped up spots in the Chase for the Sprint Cup.

Kenseth remains the top driver without a victory in the standings, but he dropped to fifth place. If the regular season ended now, the last four drivers in the Chase would be Kenseth, Ryan Newman, Clint Bowyer and Greg Biffle.

Bowyer and Biffle both moved ahead of rookie Kyle Larson, whose car caught fire against the wall just before the halfway point. Larson ended up 43rd.

Bowyer finished sixth but sounded concerned about his situation.

"We're behind, there's no question. We just did what we needed to do today," he said. "Right now, everything has to be perfect to get a decent finish and today everything was perfect. This is a tricky part of the season. Everybody is pushing hard."

THIRST FOR FUN AT DELAWARE BREWERY
Milton, Delaware, Thursday, August 21, 2014

Jeff Gordon may as well have been any average sports fan, sliding up to the bar and ordering a beer.

But for a guy who has mastered winemaking as well as he has winning races, Gordon needed a remedial course on the finer points of handling a cold one.

"Do you smell the beer like you do with wine," Gordon asked.

He raised the glass to his nose, inhaled the fruity complexity and pungent hoppiness of a Dogfish Head 61, and started to drink.

One sip turned into two sips. And with a few more swigs, Gordon was suddenly the Delaware version of TV barfly Norm Peterson.

"I could drink this all day," Gordon said, to the delight of the Dogfish Head staff.

Gordon has been soaked in champagne in Victory Lane three times this season. He's sipped wine from his private stock at Jeff Gordon Cellars.

After a personal tour of one of the top craft breweries in the business, Gordon was willing to make 24 stand for more than the number on his car - he could use a case of the good stuff to lug back to North Carolina.

"I think I have a new appreciation for a good beer," Gordon said, laughing.

Gordon has had plenty of hops in his step this year, enjoying a career renaissance with Hendrick Motorsports that has him with three wins and a spot in the Chase for the Sprint Cup championship field. He's coming off a win Sunday at Michigan International Speedway that thrust him to the top of the points standings. Gordon, who fueled retirement talk at the Daytona 500, has backtracked from any thoughts about hanging up the helmet.

He looks every bit a title contender - and his cars are as stout as some of the dark, roasty and complex beers Dogfish stirs up.

"I feel like we're the best team," Gordon said Wednesday.

So do the folks at Dogfish Brewery.

Gordon toured the brewery (with beer in hand) and lunched at the brewpub (complete with a five-beer sampling flight) to promote the September 28 race at Dover International Speedway.

Dogfish is widely considered the top of the field, the Jimmie Johnson of the east coast craft beer scene. It's No. 1 and always the beer to beat. Victory Brewing, Yards Brewing and Flying Fish would make up the rest of what could be considered the Hendrick Motorsports of craft beers.

Gordon seemed as interested in the ingredients that go into brewing beers as most fans would be at an inside racing tour at the Hendrick shop.

Forget fuel tanks. Tanks and tanks of beers, enough to satisfy the palate of all the race fans at Dover, filled the brewery.

Dogfish founder Sam Calagione led Gordon on a personal tour of the complex and they startled the rest of the public who had their routine stroll turn into so much more. Many fans were left with their mouths agape when the four-time NASCAR champion walked by with his safety goggles on.

"I had no idea he'd be here," said fan Gary Cancrow, who snapped a quick picture. "He's my favorite driver, too."

Gordon found some comparisons between a successful brewery and a race team.

"When I look at this, I think somebody's going to buy that beer, or buy that by the case, and for us, we have a facility that buys our engines and engine parts but we don't link it to a person, we link it to a performance," Gordon said.

Calagione said Hendrick and Dogfish always had to be at their best to stay on top.

"I'd say both of our company's are equally obsessed with engineering and performance," he said. "Ours is a lot more based with smaller customers while Jeff is all about sponsors."

For all the star power Gordon brought to Delaware, he was only the second most famous celebrity to tour the brewery. Former Led Zeppelin singer Robert Plant found a whole lotta love with the beer when he notched his name as Dogfish's head frontman.

Gordon is again a contender to win this weekend at Bristol. He wins at Kansas and the Brickyard 400 to go along with Michigan. He has 91 career wins and his fantastic season has put 100 in sight.

"It's great to play a role in the results on Sundays and know my guys believe in me," he said.

He's again established himself as a top contender for the championship, and his first in the Chase era.

Retire? Maybe if his achy back finally gives out for him. But he expected to have a longer shelf life than any mass produced beer.

"I don't believe in retirement," Gordon said. "I believe in the next step in life."

Against the backdrop of local favorites like Shrimpys Snack Shack and Go Fish, Gordon made it down to the boardwalk to meet about 300 fans for a Q&A. The Delaware natives had little use for Gordon's thoughts on the revamped Chase or night racing at Dover. They wanted to know, what about some Dogfish sponsorship on the No. 24 Chevrolet?

Pennsylvania-based Yeungling Brewery has stepped up of late for Austin Dillon. But Dogfish wasn't willing to spend the big bucks on Gordon, yet.

"I don't know if we can hang with that," Calagione said.

Gordon skipped the beer to dump a bucket of ice water over Calagione's head as part of the Ice Bucket Challenge. Gordon brought wine from his private stock, swapping some cabernet and chardonnay from 2007 (of his Ella label) and 2010s (of son, Leo) for some Delaware beer.

Gordon preferred the Namaste, a Belgian wit crafted with oranges, lemongrass, coriander and peppercorns.

Sounds good, especially after a victory.

But Gordon wasn't ready to commit to home brewing quite yet.

"The beer business would have been fun to get into," Gordon said. "But I like wine."

GORDON COVETS ELUSIVE 5TH TITLE
Joliet, Illinois, Saturday, September 13, 2014

Jeff Gordon hopped off a plane, his typical polished self, ready for a full day of appearances to promote NASCAR's championship race. Then he glanced down at his black polo and saw for the first time the thick, white streaks of deodorant that had soiled his shirt.

"What a rookie move!" he crowed before he bee-lined for the closest bathroom.

Gordon had been rushed that morning. His wife, Ingrid, had been in New York City at Fashion Rocks, and the NASCAR superstar was home alone with his two small children. It made for a frenzied morning of getting Ella and Leo up and out the door to school, while also getting himself ready for a whirlwind media tour through Toronto.

The end result was a shirt stained with deodorant streaks on a driver known for an aplomb that made him the first NASCAR star to dazzle the suits on Madison Ave.

The height of his success was almost 20 years ago, when a young Gordon collected 40 wins in four seasons and won championships in 1995, 1997 and 1998. By the time he added his fourth championship, in 2001, Gordon could do no wrong.

He had a pretty wife, an appeal that brought in new NASCAR fans and opened doors that drivers had never been through before:

Gordon is the first and only NASCAR driver to host "Saturday Night Live."

But life has changed so much in the 13 years since. Gordon went through a public divorce, eventually remarried and started a family. And on the track, well, the wins were no longer so easy.

Now, at 43 years old, his passion for racing and winning has been revived. Gordon wants nothing more than to win his fifth series title - the Chase for the Sprint Cup championship begins Sunday at Chicagoland Speedway - and he has the full support of his family in chasing his goal. When Ingrid, who didn't know Gordon when he was an annual threat for the championship, asked him what it would take to win a title, Gordon explained that it needed his full commitment.

"Meetings and testing and being well rested, trying not to have too many distractions," Gordon said in an interview with The Associated Press. "There's a fine line between balancing that out and being a good parent and a good race car driver. Those moments come where the team schedules a test and you'd be all, 'Oh, well we had this scheduled is there any way you can move that?' But Ingrid is like 'OK, you do what you have to do.'

"When we haven't won championships, we've had conversations of 'What could I have done to help? What can the team do?' all these things, and some of those conversations lead to 'You know, there's some things that I can do that would improve my commitment to the team.'"

These weren't the kind of problems Gordon had to consider in the first half of his career. He won nearly 60 races before his 30th birthday, and really could do no wrong. He moved to Florida with his first wife and lived far away from the Hendrick Motorsports crew doing the grunt work on his race car.

"When you are winning all the time, you can get away with a lot of stuff," Gordon said. "When I moved to Florida, I'd come to the shop every couple of weeks, and people hardly ever saw me. As long as we won one every fifth race, I don't care if I don't see you again for a year."

But when the wins tapered off, the problems began.

"When you are not winning, it's all about the details, and 'Where is Jeff? Is he working as hard as we're working? Is he as committed as we are?'" Gordon said. "I don't ever want there to be questions about my commitment."

There were problems, though, particularly midway through last season when he and crew chief Alan Gustafson were at odds. They were winless, struggling to get into Chase contention, and neither was satisfied with the performance.

It took a difficult heart-to-heart talk between the two to strengthen the relationship and get the No. 24 rolling in the right direction. Gordon earned his only win last year in late October, but the team has been incredibly consistent this season. Gordon goes into the Chase tied for the second seed, with three wins this season, including a victory at Indianapolis Motor Speedway on the 20th anniversary of his win in the inaugural Brickyard 400.

Gordon led the points 17 of the 26 weeks in NASCAR's regular season and has an average finish of 10th this year.

"I've had four crew chiefs now and with all of them, I've said 'Don't treat me like I'm a multi-time champion who has won a lot. You've got to treat me like you'd treat any driver. You do what it takes. Calm me down on the radio, motivating me on the radio, off the track. Say, 'I need this out of you.' Don't hold me to a higher standard,'" Gordon said.

"And every one of them holds me to a different standard. So you have to have those moments where somebody like Alan gets to that point and says 'I've probably spoiled him a little bit, now I'm mad, now we need to have a conversation.'"

That was the turning point for Gordon and his team, and his confidence has been soaring all season. He is certain he is a viable threat to win this championship.

Only Gordon has never won in the Chase format - all his titles came under the old straight points system - and this year's format has been dramatically overhauled. There are three rounds of eliminations that will set up a four-driver shootout in November's season finale.

He's always believed that no matter the format, the best team wins, and Gordon is adamant that title belongs to him this year.

"I've never wanted anything more than this," he said. "Partially because it's eluded me. I've pretty much done everything in this sport except for winning Kentucky, and maybe I don't have seven or eight championships, but my bucket list is the Sprint Cup, under this format, to prove to myself and others that we can do it."

Gordon joked at the start of the year that if he were to win the title, he'd immediately retire and go be a full-time family man. He laughs now at all the attention that comment garnered, but doesn't regret making the statement.

"My whole reason was for saying that was because I really want to win a Sprint Cup. That's how much I want to win one," he said. "If somebody told me right now, today, you can win the Sprint Cup but in your acceptance speech you have to say 'This is it for me,' I would do it. I would do it."

WIN AT DOVER IN CHASE ELIMINATION RACE
Dover, Delaware, Sunday, September 28, 2014

Jeff Gordon won the third race in the Chase for the Sprint Cup championship for an automatic spot in the 12-driver field that advanced to the next round.

Gordon was in control in the closing laps Sunday at Dover International Speedway and joined Brad Keselowski and Joey Logano as the three drivers who were guaranteed a berth in the next Chase round with victories.

"It wasn't about the points. It wasn't about just squeezing by to get to the next round," Gordon said after his fourth win of the season and 92nd overall. "It was about making a statement. I don't know how you make a bigger statement than what this team just did right there."

Kurt Busch, AJ Allmendinger, Greg Biffle and Aric Almirola were eliminated from championship contention. Four more drivers will be eliminated in the next three-race segment that starts next week at Kansas Speedway.

Kasey Kahne was the last driver to make the Chase cut. Kevin Harvick also advanced, along with Jimmie Johnson, Kyle Busch, Dale Earnhardt Jr., Matt Kenseth and Ryan Newman.

Hamlin was the lone driver of the bottom four entering Dover to race his way into the top 12. The points will reset for the Kansas, Charlotte and Talladega.

"We can beat every car on the race track. We just need some good luck," Harvick said. "If we get some luck, we'll win races and have a shot at the championship."

Kahne survived after falling two laps down and needed every point he could muster to crack the top 12.

Gordon won for the fifth time at Dover and first since 2001, leading four Hendrick Motorsports drivers into the next round.

"I don't know what I've found, but I think a lot of it has to do with (crew chief) Alan Gustafson and all the guys on this No. 24 team," Gordon said. "They've just giving me such an awesome race car team this year. I'm having so much fun."

Team Penske was rolling, winning four of the last five races dating to Bristol, including the first two Chase races. Keselowski was second at Dover to continue his strong Chase effort through three races.

Johnson, Logano and Kenseth completed the top five at Dover. Chase drivers took 11 of the top 13 spots.

Harvick led a whopping 223 laps from his seventh pole of the season until he suffered tire woes and finished 13th.

"We can beat every car on the race track. We just need some good luck," Harvick said. "If we get some luck, we'll win races and have a shot at the championship."

Kurt Busch, the 2004 Cup champion, failed to advance in his milestone 500th career start.

"It just was tight the last 100 miles," he said. "You can't expect to advance running 15th. You have to be more competitive."

Allmendinger fell two points shy of the cutoff. Busch was six off, Biffle seven and Almirola 18.

Chapter 8

GOODBYE

Jeff Gordon waves to the fans before a NASCAR Sprint Cup Series auto race in Avondale, Arizona, March 15, 2015. (AP Photo/Rick Scuteri)

2015 THE END OF HIS CAREER
Thursday, January 22, 2015

Jeff Gordon, with a nagging back injury, a young family he wanted to spend more time with and a phenom waiting in the wings at Hendrick Motorsports, knew midway through last season that he had one more year in him.

NASCAR's most charismatic driver, the man behind the wheel of the famed and sometimes feared No. 24, had decided it was time to call it quits on one of the most successful careers in motorsports history. The four-time champion conferred with Rick Hendrick, the only team owner he has had over 23 years of Sprint Cup racing, and settled on a date.

The 43-year-old Gordon announced Thursday that 2015 will be his final season as a full-time driver, saddening legions of fans, fellow drivers and others who watched him became the face of stock car racing as the sport exploded in popularity a generation ago.

In an interview with The Associated Press, Gordon said he reached his decision last summer. He had seen other drivers embark on distracting farewell tours, and he didn't want to be that guy. Although he told his crew chief of his decision after narrowly missing out on shot at a fifth championship, it took time to settle on the day to tell the world.

It started with a conversation with his two young children when they woke up for school. They worried they won't go to the race track anymore, that other kids might think of them differently if their father is not a famous race car driver.

The conversation with Ella and Leo made the decision a reality for Gordon — and he wept.

"Ella just stared at me, she'd never seen me cry like that before," Gordon told AP. "After that, I seriously broke down. It hit me like a ton of bricks, and I got so emotional and thought, 'How am I going to get through this day?'"

Gordon said he sobbed during the entire 30-minute drive to Hendrick Motorsports, where he tearfully informed his team and his longtime employees of his decision. Gordon choked back tears yet again during his interview with AP when his mother sent him a text message that he read aloud: "I never knew watching SportsCenter could be so emotional."

"I'm emotional because I am so proud," Gordon said. "It's all I ever wanted, to be a race car driver. And here I've lived this incredible dream and yet that chapter of my life has been fulfilled and it's now time to go to the next step and the next chapter."

He made a point to say he didn't use the word "retirement" because he could still drive again after this season.

Gordon's 92 wins trail only Hall of Fame drivers Richard Petty (200) and David Pearson (105). His fame reaches far beyond the track and resonates with non-sports fans. He won all the big races, collected four championships in just seven years and had 58 victories before his 30th birthday.

He was a new breed of driver when he broke into NASCAR's top series, arriving with a sprint car pedigree and talent that made him an immediate contender. The clean-cut kid helped raised NASCAR's corporate image beyond its moonshine roots, making it a legitimate power on Madison Avenue as tens of thousands of new fans flocked to automobile racing in the late 1990s and 2000s.

"Jeff changed the personality and perception of a race car driver in NASCAR," retired NASCAR crew chief Larry McReynolds said. "Before he came along, the perception was more about the good old Southeastern boy wearing blue jeans, big belt buckles and boots. But he created a new buzz in our sport because he looked like he stepped off the cover of a GQ magazine."

Gordon became such a household name that he even hosted "Saturday Night Live" and was name-dropped in a Nelly song. He did it all while dominating at the track as the "Rainbow Warrior," teaming with crew chief Ray Evernham to collect checkered flags at a record pace.

Gordon, who debuted in the final race of the 1992 season in Atlanta, won championships in 1995, 1997, 1998 and 2001. He also has three Daytona 500 victories and a record five Brickyard 400 wins. Gordon told AP that his 1994 win in the inaugural Brickyard 400 — NASCAR's first race at historic Indianapolis Motor Speedway — was easily the highlight of his career.

The low point? Intentionally wrecking Clint Bowyer in the closing laps of the 2012 race at Phoenix, where frustrations over a disappointing season got the best of him. Gordon also said a postrace melee with Brad Keselowski last November was in part triggered by his knowledge that perhaps a shot at another championship had slipped away. He was racing for the win when contact with Keselowski effectively ended his title chances. He wound up missing the four-driver championship field by a single point.

Coming so close didn't change his decision to drive only one more year, though. With an ownership stake at Hendrick, and plans to remain involved with the organization for years to come, Gordon told AP "the timeline was just right."

Gordon suffered serious issues years ago in his back, specifically his lower spine, and needed anti-inflammatory medication and workouts with a trainer to return to full strength. He drove in pain during a winless 2008 season and briefly contemplated retirement.

He also wants to focus more on his family life, which has changed dramatically over his career.

The one-time "Wonder Boy" was a mustachioed young bachelor when he entered NASCAR, and he embarked on a storybook romance with the series' leading model that led to the most high-profile marriage the sport had ever seen. Gordon and the former Brooke Sealey split in 2002. He found happiness and the desire to start a family when he married Ingrid Vandebosch in 2006.

"I want to be with my kids," he told AP. "I'm seeing them grow up before my eyes and I'm never here."

Gordon will now take one final victory lap around the circuit with drivers such as reigning Sprint Cup rookie of the year Kyle Larson, who routinely posts childhood photos of himself in Gordon gear.

"Jeff Gordon is a hero to a lot of kids, and the driver I personally looked up to as a kid," Larson said. "He's a hero of mine."

Although no replacement for Gordon has been announced, the next driver of the No. 24 will most certainly be reigning Xfinity Series champion Chase Elliott. With a full roster of four drivers, Hendrick has been handcuffed in what he can do with the 19-year-old phenom.

Gordon has won at every track on the Sprint Cup circuit except Kentucky Speedway. His four championships trail only teammate Jimmie Johnson, a six-time champ, for most among active drivers. Petty and Earnhardt each won seven.

"There's simply no way to quantify Jeff's impact," Hendrick said. "He's one of the biggest sports stars of a generation, and his contributions to the success and growth of NASCAR are unsurpassed. There's been no better ambassador for stock car racing and no greater representation of what a champion should be."

MOTORSPORTS WORLD REACTS
Thursday, January 22, 2015

Some of the reaction to four-time champion Jeff Gordon's announcement that 2015 will be his last season as a full-time NASCAR driver:

"Jeff Gordon's significance to our sport cannot be overstated. He is an incredible competitor, and a favorite of millions of fans. His contributions throughout his career to NASCAR have elevated our sport's popularity worldwide." - Lesa Kennedy France, CEO of NASCAR's sister company, International Speedway Corp.

―――

"Can't imagine being at the track without @JeffGordonWeb. I don't think I would have ever had my opportunity without Jeff paving the way." - Three-time NASCAR champion Tony Stewart (@TonyStewart) via Twitter.

―――

"He was the guy that got me to start buying souvenirs and T-shirts when I was a kid. I've always looked up to him and it's been a great honor for me to get to race against him, have battles with him, to make him mad at times on the track, but the coolest thing is that he is going out when he is on top. I think that is the hardest thing for any of us to do when we decide we are going to retire." - NASCAR driver Jamie McMurray.

―――

"Jeff Gordon is a hero to a lot of kids, and the driver I personally looked up to as a kid, especially growing up in Northern California. I raced sprint cars like he did and at a lot of the same tracks he did over the years. To hear that Jeff Gordon is retiring is big news. He's a hero of mine and I hope he stays involved with the sport." - NASCAR driver Kyle Larson.

―――

"Anyone who follows racing anywhere around the world knows the name Jeff Gordon. He is a legend in the sport and what he's been able to accomplish over his career is nothing short of amazing. I wish him all the best in his final NASCAR season." - Three-time IndyCar champion Scott Dixon.

"Jeff's accomplishments off the track are impressive, but his numbers on the track are unbelievable. I call him the 'GOAT' - the Greatest of All Time. I believe he is the greatest NASCAR driver there has ever been. What he has done outside the sport has grown the sport's popularity immensely. I give Jeff a tremendous amount of credit for the youth movement in NASCAR. A lot of people think NASCAR started in 1992 because that's when he came on the scene and brought in a new, young audience because he appealed to the 18- to 35-year-old demographic. We didn't really have a driver at the time who could do that." - Hall of Fame driver and current FOX analyst Darrell Waltrip.

"Jeff Gordon transcends NASCAR and will be celebrated as one of the greatest drivers to ever race. We have all enjoyed watching his legend grow for more than two decades, and will continue to do so during his final full-time season. His prolonged excellence and unmatched class continue to earn him the admiration of fans across the globe. Today's announcement is a bittersweet one. I'll miss his competitive fire on a weekly basis, but I am also happy for Jeff and his family as they start a new chapter. On behalf of the entire NASCAR family, I thank Jeff for his years of dedication and genuine love for this sport, and wish him the very best in his final season." - NASCAR Chairman and CEO Brian France.

"Jeff changed the personality and perception of a race car driver in NASCAR. Before he came along, the perception was more about the good old Southeastern boy wearing blue jeans, big belt buckles and boots. But he created a new buzz in our sport because he looked like he stepped off the cover of a GQ magazine." - retired NASCAR crew chief and current FOX analyst Larry McReynolds.

"I've had a lot of good times with @JeffGordonWeb and one (crap) one. Weird to think just like all the other greats, that soon he won't be there!" - NASCAR driver Clint Bowyer (@ClintBowyer) via Twitter.

"Hard to imagine this is @JeffGordonWeb last full season. Tons of respect for him and what he's accomplished thus far. A total professional." - Hendrick Motorsports teammate Dale Earnhardt Jr. (@DaleJr) via Twitter.

"Crazy to hear that @JeffGordonWeb is retiring! What an amazing career! Glad I got to race with him!" - NASCAR driver Danica Patrick (@DanicaPatrick) via Twitter.

"Grew up a @JeffGordonWeb and @markmartin fan. Been awesome to race both of them for wins. Look forward to one more year in 2015." - NASCAR driver Joey Logano (@joeylogano) via Twitter.

"Crazy... You're the man!" - Six-time NASCAR champion Jimmie Johnson (@JimmieJohnson) via Twitter.

"Very few have done as much for our sport as @JeffGordonWeb. Nothing but respect for one of the greatest that's ever raced." - NASCAR driver Regan Smith (@ReganSmith) via Twitter.

"I feel so lucky to say I have raced against my idol and favorite driver growing up @JeffGordonWeb... ready for one more year against you." - NASCAR driver AJ Allmendinger (@AJDinger) via Twitter.

"Congrats bud @JeffGordonWeb, looking forward to seeing you kick butt one more time. Looking forward to 2015." - Former Gordon crew chief Ray Evernham (@RayEvernham) via Twitter.

"I've known Jeff since he was a teenager with a really bad mustache. It has been thrilling to watch him develop from a promising Busch Series driver into perhaps the greatest professional our sport has ever seen. Jeff showed last season that he still has a burning desire to win races and championships. You won't find a finer professional, person or charitable athlete. We have been fortunate to be associated with him for all of these years. I'm sure all fans, even of the other drivers, will want to show their appreciation to Jeff this year." - Texas Motor Speedway President Eddie Gossage.

"We got to know him when he drove with us back in 2007. He's just such a normal guy and humble guy, brilliant driver. He is a very special kind of driver. He speaks well and does all the right things. His hair is always perfect. We mocked him because of his stupid helmet with all these flames on it and he really just couldn't believe we didn't like the helmet." - IMSA team owner Wayne Taylor, who had Gordon drive for him in the 2007 Rolex 24 at Daytona.

"A true gentleman, a true team player. He was so humble. He was a champ so we thought, 'Oh, man, this guy.' But he was just normal, down to the ground, stayed at the same hotel as ours." - Driver Max Angelelli, who finished third with Gordon in the 2007 Rolex 24.

IMAGE NOT ALWAYS POLISHED AND PERFECT
Daytona Beach, Florida, Thursday, January 22, 2015

It seemed fitting that Jeff Gordon wore a tailored suit to tell his Hendrick Motorsports team and long-time employees Thursday that 2015 would be his last full-time season in NASCAR.

After all, Gordon helped transform NASCAR's image from a bunch of good ol' boys chasing each other around a track for a couple hundred bucks into a corporate giant that filled grandstands, appealed to the masses and made drivers and owners millionaires.

Gordon's legacy surely will include how he became a model spokesman for the sport, a guy who could sell himself to fans as well as Wall Street. He graced the cover of GQ magazine, hosted "Saturday Night Live" and sat in with Regis Philbin for an episode of "Live with Regis."

"It's not something that I set out to do it that way," Gordon said. "I wanted to show up today to show everybody how serious I am about this and what it means to me. This is the way I want to present myself. That goes into the mindset I've had for years to the way I approach it.

"I take it very seriously and work very hard at it, and I try to stay very focused. That's just who I am. It's contributed to a lot of the success and maybe to transcending the sport. I always try to do my best and to represent myself, my team and my sponsors in the best way that I could."

But Gordon hasn't been that way forever.

Former NASCAR and IndyCar driver John Andretti recalled a story Thursday about the first time he met Gordon — and the future four-time Cup champion looked far from ready for Corporate America.

"When I met him, he was going to IndyCar. He really wanted to talk about IndyCar," Andretti said. "There's a photo of him sitting in the Porsche IndyCar I was driving and me talking to him about it, and he was not dressed properly. Matter of fact, I told his car owner, 'The first thing you need to do is dress him." He was wearing cutoff jeans and a T-shirt. He looked like he was going dirt riding."

That was in 1990, the same year he made his stock car debut. Said Andretti: "It wasn't like he was someone you could walk up to (legendary IndyCar team owner) Roger Penske and say, 'Hey, here's your new guy.'"

HE PAVED (DIRT) ROADS FOR NASCAR HOPEFULS
Daytona Beach, Florida, Thursday, January 22, 2015

Jeff Gordon blazed a trail — a dirt-covered path, really — for NASCAR hopefuls everywhere.

Gordon, who announced Thursday that 2015 would be his final season in a full-time ride, was one of the first sprint cup drivers to make the leap to NASCAR's top series and opened the door for others to follow.

Tony Stewart, Ryan Newman, Casey Mears, Kasey Kahne, AJ Allmendinger, Clint Bowyer, Jamie McMurray and Kyle Larson are among the many NASCAR regulars who followed Gordon's route from sprint cars to stock cars.

"I don't think I would have ever had my opportunity without Jeff paving the way," Stewart posted on his Twitter page.

Gordon made his NASCAR debut in 1990. He made his Cup debut two years later, ended up in Victory Lane for the first time in 1994 and claimed his first of four titles the following year. Dirt-track drivers from coast to coast took notice.

"He was the guy that got me to start buying souvenirs and T-shirts when I was a kid," McMurray said. "I've always looked up to him and it's been a great honor for me to get to race against him, have battles with him, to make him mad at times on the track, but the coolest thing is that he is going out when he is on top. I think that is the hardest thing for any of us to do when we decide we are going to retire."

When asked how he wants his career to be defined, Gordon downplayed how much he's done for auto racing and said he would be happy "if people recognize me as a great race car driver because that's all I really wanted to be."

"It's about seeing a kid's dream become real life in front of thousands, if not, millions of people," he added.

But his colleagues see things differently.

"He did a lot for short-track racing," former NASCAR and IndyCar driver John Andretti said. "It opened up the eyes again. Ken Schrader started that. Now, there are a bunch of guys that came straight from dirt tracks that really nobody would have ever looked at, open-wheel dirt-track racing, and that has really created a new avenue for car owners to look for and also drivers to reach the big time.

"(Gordon's) legacy is opening a lot of doors and then keeping them open."

FINAL LAP FOR 'FOUR-TIME'
Charlotte, North Carolina, Sunday, June 28, 2015

Jeff Gordon never wanted a farewell tour.

Well, too bad. The four-time NASCAR champion is getting one anyway.

Since announcing in late January that this would be his final year as a full-time driver, the 44-year-old Gordon has been getting showered with souvenirs just about every week on the Sprint Cup circuit. And he's making headlines for more than just all those parting gifts.

Here's a look at Gordon's year, which includes a 10th straight berth in the Chase for the Sprint Cup championship:

January 22: Announces he's stepping away from his full-time ride in the No. 24 Chevrolet for Hendrick Motorsports, effective at the end of this season. "I've lived this incredible dream and yet that chapter of my life has been fulfilled and it's now time to go to the next step and the next chapter," Gordon said.

January 29: Hendrick announces that 19-year-old Chase Elliott, the reigning Xfinity Series champion, will replace Gordon in the Sprint Cup Series in 2016. Gordon admits there had been pressure on him from Hendrick to set a timeline on his future because the organization was looking to make long-term plans for son of 1988 champion Bill Elliott.

February 12: Says this will be his final Daytona 500 and adds that he wants no part of restrictor-plate races beyond 2015 because the risks outweigh the rewards.

Jeff Gordon answers questions at NASCAR media day at Daytona International Speedway in Daytona Beach, Florida, February 12, 2015. (AP Photo/John Raoux)

February 14: Finishes seventh in NASCAR's first race of 2015, the exhibition Sprint Unlimited at Daytona.

February 15: Wins the pole for his final Daytona 500, securing the top spot in a wild and wacky qualifying format that prompted NASCAR to tweak its qualifying procedures for restrictor-plate tracks.

February 19: Finishes second to teammate Dale Earnhardt Jr. in Budweiser Duel 1, the first of two qualifying races for the Daytona 500.

February 22: Leads a race-high 87 laps in the Daytona 500 and is out front at the halfway mark. But finishes 33rd after wrecking on the final lap. Also films a really cool "Unfinished Business" skit with actor Vince Vaughn.

Ricky Stenhouse Jr. (17), Paul Menard (27), Jeff Gordon (24), Matt Crafton (18), Trevor Bayne (6), Regan Smith (41), AJ Allmendinger (47) and Reed Sorenson (44) collide in the back stretch on the final lap of the Daytona 500 NASCAR Sprint Cup series auto race at Daytona International Speedway, February 22, 2015. (AP Photo/Phelan M. Ebenhack)

February 27: Atlanta Motor Speedway gives Gordon a maroon and yellow bandolero for Gordon's kids, Ella and Leoa, as well as a framed replica of this year's souvenir program featuring the four-time champ and signed by the track staff. Track paints "Thanks 24" on the grass and plans to make the scoring tower all 24s on the 24th lap of the race.

March 1: Crashes hard into a concrete wall along the backstretch at Atlanta, hitting a section unprotected by an energy-absorbing SAFER barrier. He finishes 41st. The wreck comes a week after Kyle Busch smashed headfirst into an unprotected wall during the Xfinity Series race at Daytona, leaving him with a broken right leg and left foot. Gordon escapes without injury and says afterward that he "can't believe it. That's amazing to me. Anyway. Hopefully now that will get fixed."

March 6: Gets emotional as Las Vegas Motor Speedway officials present him a custom blackjack table with images of his No. 24 car on the felt surface. Track also displays massive sign atop Turn 4 grandstands that reads: "Thank You Jeff 24." Later, wins first pole at Vegas.

March 7: Crashes pole-winning car in the last 30 seconds of the final practice in Vegas, forcing him to a backup car and sending him to the rear of the field to start the race.

March 8: Finishes 18th at Las Vegas Motor Speedway, marking the first time in his illustrious career that he failed to crack the top 15 in the first three races of the season.

March 10: Meets with NASCAR executives in hopes of getting timeline on when energy-absorbing SAFER barriers will be fully installed at every track.

March 12: Begins appearance in Dallas by burning circles in the middle of a freeway with John Godwin of "Duck Dynasty" riding shotgun. Texas Motor Speedway later presents Gordon with a Texas-shaped victory lane paver from his 2009 win at the track, and former Cowboys cornerback Everson Walls gives him a No. 24 "Gordon" Cowboys jersey. Gordon also eases up on NASCAR after discussing track safety issues with officials behind closed doors. He says he may have prematurely questioned NASCAR's plans for installing SAFER barriers after his violent crash at Atlanta Motor Speedway.

March 15: Phoenix International Raceway posts yellow 24 speed limit signs throughout the grounds, passes out 24 tribute towels to fans to wave on lap 24, paints a 24 on the infield and invites fans to write notes to Gordon on the start/finish line prior to the race. Gordon later finishes a season-best ninth.

March 18: Auto Club displays Historic Route 24 on roads leading into the track.

March 19: Appears on "American Idol" to ask finalists to sing the national anthem before Sunday's race at Fontana and deliver the "drivers, start your engines" command.

March 22: Auto Club Speedway in Fontana, California, gives Gordon a commemorative helmet. He later finishes 10th for his second straight top-10 showing.

March 29: Rallies to finish ninth at Martinsville Speedway, but his third consecutive top 10 was bittersweet because it could have ended in victory lane. Gordon, who started fourth, took the lead with 58 laps remaining and looked to be in control until he was caught speeding on pit road. The mistake put him at the back of the pack. He charged through the field over the final 40 laps -- showing some vintage Gordon moves -- but knew he ruined what could have been a memorable day. "Oh, my gosh, I'm so disappointed," he said. "I don't even know what to say right now."

April 2: His two children are named grand marshals for the Sprint Cup race at Bristol Motor Speedway. Ella Gordon, 7, and her 4-year-old brother Leo will give the command to start the Food City 500 on April 19.

April 6: Takes his wife and their two kids to the 137th annual White House Easter egg roll. Also appears on "Live with Kelly and Michael," where he takes part in the GimmeFive Challenge that encourages children to come up with five ways to live healthier lives. Gordon does five push-ups on stage and then challenges Hendrick Motorsports teammate Dale Earnhardt Jr. to do five squat jumps.

April 10: Makes TV analyst debut during the Xfinity Series race at Texas Motor Speedway. Gordon provided his insight for Fox Sports, offering a glimpse at what his future might hold after he steps away from full-time driving duties.

April 11: Gambles by taking two tires on final pit stop and finishes seventh at Texas Motor Speedway.

April 12: Attends the popular music festival Coachella in Indio, California. Gordon and his wife catch concerts by acts like Florence + the Machine, Kaskade and David Guetta at the six-stage festival that has become a hot spot for celebrities.

April 19: Rallies from two laps down to finish a season-best third at Bristol Motor Speedway. Gordon welcomes the podium finish "because I didn't have a shot at winning." The better part of the day happens when Gordon's kids, Ella and Leo, serve as grand marshals and give the command to start engines. "Highlight for me," Gordon said. "The day couldn't be bad after that. That was so, so cool, and they nailed it. I'm just so, so proud of them. ... They just had a blast preparing for it, just practicing in the car on the way to school. So funny. And Leo, he had to put his little engine rev in there at the end, which I thought just kind of put it over the top. As soon as the red flag came, I went back to the bus and rewound it and watched it with them, and they were just beaming. It was awesome."

April 26: Notches sixth consecutive top-10 finish with an eighth-place showing at Richmond International Raceway.

April 29: Gets named honorary pace-car driver for the Indianapolis 500. A five-time Brickyard 400 winner who grew up in Indiana, Gordon will enjoy pre-race festivities May 24 before getting behind the wheel of the Corvette pace car and leading the field to the green flag. He'll stay for a few laps and then fly to Charlotte, North Carolina, to compete in the Coca-Cola 600 later that night. Gordon's version of the "double" surely will be a special moment in his farewell tour.

May 2: Claims 80th pole of career, and jokes afterward that a rare trip with friends to Talladega's infamous infield boulevard the night before helped him turn the fastest lap in qualifying.

May 3: Finishes a disappointing 31st at Talladega Superspeedway, ending a six-race streak of top-10 showings, after a late mistake. Gordon gets caught speeding on pit road during the final stops, dropping him from near the front of the field to the back of the pack. It's especially frustrating considering he started on the pole and teammates Dale Earnhardt Jr. and Jimmie Johnson came home 1-2 for Hendrick Motorsports. "You want to seize those opportunities," Gordon said. "This was an opportunity for us. We had an awesome race car. I definitely feel like we had the best car. Junior was good. Jimmie was good. But I felt like we were amazing."

May 9: Crosses the finish line fourth in the rain-delayed race at Kansas Speedway, chasing Hendrick Motorsports teammates Jimmie Johnson and Dale Earnhardt Jr. over the final few laps.

May 16: Driving in his 23rd consecutive and maybe final All-Star race, Gordon finishes fourth -- his best showing at the non-points event since 2006.

May 21: Reveals he has signed a multi-year contract with Fox to work as a full-time NASCAR race analyst in 2016, teaming with Mike Joy and Darrell Waltrip in the network's three-man booth. His first race will be February at Daytona International Speedway. He will replace Larry McReynolds, who will move to an in-race analyst role alongside Michael Waltrip and host Chris Myers. "NASCAR has provided me so many incredible memories, experiences and opportunities throughout my 23 years as a driver, and I can't wait to start a new chapter in racing with this new relationship with Fox," Gordon says. "I feel so lucky to be a part of a sport that I'm very passionate about, and now I get the opportunity to share that passion to millions of race fans from a whole new perspective."

May 24: Driving a Corvette pace car, Gordon leads the field to the green flag at the prestigious Indy 500. Gordon pulls off his own version of "the double" by starting the day in Indy -- he watches the first few -- and then traveling to Charlotte, North Carolina, for the Coca-Cola 600. Gordon finishes 15th at Charlotte Motor Speedway. "I accomplished more than I ever hoped to in racing, but one thing that eluded me that we pursued — my dad, my mom and myself — was getting a chance to race the Indianapolis 500," says Gordon, a five-time NASCAR winner at Indianapolis Motor Speedway. "And I've said before, winning the inaugural Brickyard 400 fulfilled that dream."

Pace car driver Jeff Gordon, left, talks with former Indy 500 champion Dario Franchitti before driving the pace car for the 99th running of the Indianapolis 500 auto race at Indianapolis Motor Speedway, May 24, 2015. (AP Photo/Darron Cummings)

May 31: Steadily improves throughout race and finishes 10th at Dover International Speedway -- Gordon's eighth top-10 showing in the last 10 races of this season.

June 7: Has a heated exchanged with crew chief Alan Gustafson on the radio before finishing 14th at Pocono Raceway. "It's intense out there," Gordon says later. "We had a better car than what we finished. I would say a little bit of build up with the type of season that we have had so far. It seems like every time we have a car that is capable of either winning or running in the top five, something takes us out of it. At that point, I think both Alan and I were frustrated."

June 12: Phoenix International Speedway announces it will rename itself "Jeff Gordon Raceway" for its November 15 race. Gordon told track officials that "this has been a very special year, especially as it relates to the fans and the tracks. You guys took it to a whole other level."

June 14: Finishes 21st and a lap down at the rain-shortened race at Michigan International Speedway. Gordon starts and stays in the top 10 early, but fades after two pit-road issues. First, Ryan Blaney forces Gordon into a pit-road barrier. Then, Gordon has to re-pit after his team fails to secure three lug nuts on his front-left wheel.

June 20: With his wife, two children and parents in tow, Gordon visits the quarter-midget track in Rio Linda, California, where he started racing. Sonoma Raceway put together the reunion tour in advance of Gordon's final race at his home track. Gordon later stops at his old middle school in Vallejo, then holds a birthday party for daughter Ella before the family heads off for a camping trip in Vancouver. "I try to hold back, but I don't have that switch that turns it off and on when a moment affects me," Gordon says. "Being here, having my parents here, seeing it come full circle and have my kids here, it's emotional."

Jeff Gordon shows his children, Ella and Leo, around Roy Hayer Memorial Speedway in Rio Linda, California. Gordon began his career at the quarter-midget dirt track when he was 5 and the track was called Cracker Jack Track, June 20, 2015. (AP Photo/Jenna Fryer)

June 26: Sonoma presents Gordon with a Melchior bottle of wine, which has a rendering of his famed No. 24 DuPont Chevrolet, the years of his five wins at the road course and the title "Hometown Hero" on it. Gordon grew up in northern California before his family moved to Indiana to bolster his racing career.

June 28: Drops to the back of the pack because of pit-road penalty late, works way up to third with eight laps to go and then fades to a 16th-place finish at Sonoma Raceway.

June 30: The Ride of Fame presents Gordon with his very own double-decker bus to honor his farewell season. The ceremony at Pier 78 in New York City includes the unveiling of a permanent decal bearing Gordon's image on the front of the bus. Other athletes inducted into the Ride of Fame include New York Yankees reliever Mariano Rivera, Washington Capitals star Alex Ovechkin and New York Rangers goalie Henrik Lundqvist. Gordon is the first racecar driver to be inducted.

July 5: Gets tangled in a harrowing wreck near the finish line that sends Austin Dillon's car sailing into the Daytona International Speedway catch-fence and causing a few minor injuries to spectators. Gordon crosses the line sixth in his final race at Daytona, notching his ninth top-10 finish of the season. Hours before the race, speedway officials handed out thousands of placards showing pictures that commemorate Gordon's milestones at Daytona. Fans waved them during driver introductions. "I have this feeling it's going to hit me all at once at Homestead," Gordon says, referring to the season finale at Homestead.

July 10: Kentucky Speedway gives Gordon 96 commemorative bottles of bourbon -- 24 from each of the four master distilleries.

July 11: Finishes seventh at Kentucky Speedway, the only NASCAR track at which Gordon has failed to win during his illustrious career. He now has 10 top-10s this season.

July 19: Holds on for another top-10 finish, crossing the line ninth at New Hampshire Motor Speedway. His final race at the track takes place September 27, the second leg of the Chase for the Sprint Cup championship. Gordon currently sits 10th in points, but needs a victory to lock up a Chase spot.

July 23: His parents, friends and even some former high school teachers are among hundreds of people lining the streets in Pittsboro, Indiana, for Jeff Gordon Day. The police chief names Gordon an honorary police officer and presents him a real badge. School officials give Gordon a plaque of the diploma he earned in 1989 with an inscription that reads in part: "to our most famous graduate." And Indiana Gov. Mike Pence presents Gordon with the Sagamore of the Wabash award -- the highest state honor for a civilian. "This has been one of the best days of my life and I say that sincerely," Gordon says, his voice cracking. "I not only get to see what Pittsboro's meant to me, I get to see what Pittsboro's meant to you by the way you've come out and supported me. This to me is a very, very special day."

Jeff Gordon, left, waves to fans along the parade route in Pittsboro, as part of his farewell tour, July 23, 2015. (AP Photo/Michael Conroy)

July 26: Crashes on lap 50 in his final Brickyard 400 and finishes a season-worst 42nd, ending his shot at a second consecutive and record sixth win at Indianapolis Motor Speedway. It's also his worst showing in a Sprint Cup race since 2008. "It's not the way we want our day to go here," Gordon says. The fans don't care, chanting "Jeff! Jeff!" as he walks off the track for the final time.

July 31: As its parting gift to Gordon, Pocono donates $24,000 to the Jeff Gordon Children's Foundation.

August 2: Runs in the middle of the pack most of the day but ends up tying his season-best finish with a third-place showing at Pocono Raceway. Gordon passes several cars that run out of gas in the closing laps for his third top-five of the year and first since finishing fourth at Kansas in May.

August 4: Celebrates his 44th birthday.

August 9: Deals with a brake-line issue early, loses four laps repairing the problem and never recovers at Watkins Glen International. He finishes 41st -- his worst career finish at the track where he once won three consecutive Cup races (1997-99). "Right now, I just feel like we can't afford to have these kinds of finishes if we are going to make the Chase," says Gordon, who falls from 10th to 12th in the points standings.

August 12: Raises money for children's cancer research by taking part in the Kick-It charity race at Slideways Karting in Iowa. Gordon is joined by fellow NASCAR drivers Kasey Kahne, Tony Stewart and Kyle Larson.

August 14: To commemorate his final race at Michigan, track officials give Gordon and his family a vacation at the iconic Grand Hotel on Mackinac Island, Michigan. The track paints "24" in the tri-oval grass and plans to give away 1,000 "24" foam fingers at pre-race driver introductions.

August 16: Restarts 10th with 16 laps to go, but fades to a 17th-place finish at Michigan International Speedway. Gordon also falls one spot to 13th in the point standings. Because he remains winless on the season, Gordon ranks 15th in the projected 16-driver Chase field and needs solid results over the final three races of the regular season to make the Chase.

August 21: Bristol unveils plans for "Jeff Gordon Terrace," a section of seats renamed to honor the five-time Bristol champion. Jeff Gordon Terrace will open in 2016 and be located in sections now known as Junior Johnson Terrace and Cale Yarborough Terrace. Jeff Gordon Terrace will be located above Junior Johnson and Cale Yarborough terraces and below Dale Earnhardt Terrace. "You deserve to be among the legends here at Bristol," track general manager Jerry Caldwell tells Gordon.

August 22: Driving a car with a throwback, rainbow-colored paint scheme, Gordon finishes four laps down in 20th at Bristol Motor Speedway. Gordon deals with several tire/wheel issues, forcing him to make green-flag pit stops and lose valuable spots on the half-mile track.

September 4: Darlington gives Gordon a painting depicting scenes from each of his seven victories as the track nicknamed "Too Tough to Tame." Gordon has four more wins at the famed track than his nearest competitor.

September 6: Starts fifth and runs in the top 10 most of the night, but fails to make up ground after a final pit stop and finishes 16th in the Southern 500 at Darlington Raceway, the track where Gordon has seven career wins. Gordon ranks 15th in the projected Chase field.

September 7: Chase scenarios released, and Gordon will clinch a spot in the 16-driver field by finishing 17th or better at Richmond International Raceway. He needs to finish 18th if he leads a lap and 19th if he leads the most laps. He also clinches automatically if there's a repeat winner at Richmond.

September 11: In honor of Gordon's final race at Richmond, track officials donate a NASCAR toy box and portable DVDs players to children's hospitals in Gordon's name.

September 12: Safely makes the Chase with a seventh-place finish at Richmond International Raceway. Gordon enters the Chase in 13th position in the 16-driver field. "This has not been the best year so far," Gordon says. "It would have been pretty disappointing in my final year not to be in the Chase. This feels really good."

September 15: NHRA star John Force says thanks to Gordon by unveiling a tribute paint scheme for the Carolina Nationals, which begin in three days.

September 16: Spends part of the day in New York City to promote the Chase. Gordon visits "Good Morning America" and later cooks with celebrity chef Rachael Ray.

September 20: Restarts second with five laps to go at Chicagoland Speedway, but fades and finishes 14th in the first of 10 Chase races. Ranks 12th in Chase standings.

September 27: Becomes NASCAR's newest "Iron Man" by starting his 789th consecutive race, breaking the previous record held by Ricky Rudd. Rudd broke Terry Labonte's streak of 655 consecutive starts in 2002 and then extended the mark to 788 in 2005. Gordon's streak began with his Cup debut at Atlanta Motor Speedway in 1992. He hasn't missed a race since. Should Gordon make every start the rest of the season, he'll end his career with 797 straight starts. To commemorate the milestone, Gordon and his family took a parade lap around New Hampshire Motor Speedway in a duck boat usually reserved for Boston's champions.

September 27: Finishes seventh at New Hampshire Motor Speedway and moves up to 10th in the Chase standings. Gordon is the only driver to compete in all 41 Cup races at NHMS and leads all drivers in top-five finishes, top-10s, laps led and laps completed at the 1.058-mile track.

October 2: Dover International Speedway presents Gordon, a five-time winner at the Monster Mile, with 90 miniature Miles the Monster trophies for his entire No. 24 team and his family. "I don't know how we're going to get all those home," Gordon says. Gordon also gets proclamations from the city of Dover and Delaware's House of Representatives and Senate. Gordon's last win came at Dover last year, so it could stand as the final victory of his career unless he wins one of the next eight races.

October 4: Runs in the top 10 most of the day before finishing 12th at Dover International Speedway. It's good enough to advance to the 12-man Contender round of the Chase.

October 11: Steadily improves all race and winds up eighth at Charlotte Motor Speedway, site of the first race in the Contender round of the Chase.

October 17: Kansas Speedway President Pat Warren presents Gordon with a replica of his first quarter-midget race car. The speedway is known for giving away pedal cars to pole winners, so Warren reached out to students at North Kansas City Technical School in Missouri with his unique idea. The students spent nights and weekends perfecting the project, which is a slightly smaller version of Gordon's first race car in 1977. He called it "The Fuzz Car."

October 18: Fades from sixth to 24th early in the race but finds a way to come home 10th at Kansas Speedway, leaving him in good position to advance to the Eliminator round. He calls the run "absolutely horrible." "We were absolutely as far off as you can be," he says. "That's one of the hardest top 10s I've ever had to go through. I'm proud of the team. They fought hard, and that's why we're where we are, but, God, it was ugly."

October 21: Takes his daughter, Ella, to see pop star Taylor Swift in concert in Greensboro, North Carolina.

October 25: Starts from the pole at Talladega Superspeedway, runs mostly in the top 10 and then finishes third in the final restrictor-plate race of his career. Gordon advances to the eight-man Eliminator round, where he's the only driver without a victory this season. "You can't count us out, especially when you look at the tracks in the Eliminator round," he says.

Crew members change the tires and refuel Sprint Cup Series driver Jeff Gordon's car during the NASCAR Sprint Cup Series auto race at Talladega Superspeedway, October 25, 2015. (AP Photo/Mark Almond)

October 30: Martinsville Speedway President Clay Campbell presents Gordon with an eight-car train, one for each of his wins at the Virginia track.

November 1: Gordon receives the H. Clay Earles Award, given for "outstanding dedication to auto racing." The award is named after Earles, the founder of Martinsville Speedway. Gordon is an eight-time winner at Martinsville. "It's really special, especially knowing they don't give that out every year," he says. "I'm honored. I love this place. The family has been so good to this sport, so good to me." Former NASCAR President Bill France Jr. was the first recipient of the award in 2000.

November 1: Wins for the first time in his final season, clinching a spot in the Chase championship by taking the checkered flag at Martinsville Speedway after Matt Kenseth intentionally wrecks leader Joey Logano. Gordon calls the victory "one of my finest moments I've ever had." Gordon celebrates by jumping along the track like a kid on Christmas and then climbing into the grandstands to hang with fans. "I don't know what it feels like to be a rock star, but that's as close as it can get," Gordon says. "That's a rock star moment right there." His 93rd career victory means he will be one of four drivers racing for the title at Homestead-Miami Speedway in three weeks. Gordon's last championship came in 2001.

November 6: Texas Motor Speedway gives Gordon two ponies and an original painting as going-away gifts. Track president Eddie Gossage also presents Gordon with custom-made cowboy boots and a replica of the Gordon Road street sign on the property. Gossage shows Gordon the custom mural that is still being painted and then brings Scout and Smoky, a pair of Shetland ponies, into the media center. Gordon says his kids are "going to flip out." The track displays Gordon's famed No. 24 all around the track along with a logo for "Jeff Gordon's Last Rodeo."

Jeff Gordon, second from left, laughs after Texas Motor Speedway president Eddie Gossage presented Gordon with two ponies during a NASCAR Sprint Cup auto race availability in the media center at Texas Motor Speedway, November 6, 2015. (AP Photo/LM Otero)

November 8: Runs in the top 10 for the final third of the race and finishes ninth at Texas Motor Speedway, his 19th top-10 of the season.

November 14: NASCAR media members present Gordon with something he doesn't have -- a trophy from Kentucky Speedway. It's the lone track at which Gordon never won, so reporters came up with gag gift to say thanks for being such a class act to deal with for more than two decades.

November 15: Places sixth in the rain-shortened race at Jeff Gordon Raceway. Yes, Phoenix International Raceway renames the track in honor of Gordon's final race.

CITATIONS AND BYLINES

FIFTH CHAMPIONSHIP THREAT
Charlotte, North Carolina, Wednesday, July 7, 2004
By Jenna Fryer

SIGNS OF OLD DOMINANCE
Wednesday, August 11, 2004
By Mike Harris

HENDRICK PLANE CRASHES
Martinsville, Virginia, Monday, October 25, 2004
By Hank Kurz, Jr.

WITH HEAVY HEARTS IT'S BACK TO WORK
Hampton, Georgia, Saturday, October 30, 2004
By Paul Newberry

FINAL WEEK OF THE CHASE
Charlotte, North Carolina, Wednesday, November 17, 2004
By Jenna Fryer

GORDON AND JOHNSON FALL SHORT
Homestead, Florida, Monday, November 22, 2004
By Tim Reynolds

FANS 'SALUTE' GORDON AT TALLADEGA
Talladega, Alabama, Monday, April 30, 2007
By Jenna Fryer

GORDON MORE LIKE ERNHARDT THAN FANS ADMIT
Talladega, Alabama, Monday, April 30, 2007
By Jenna Fryer

WILLING TO TAKE RISKS FOR MORE WINS
Talladega, Alabama, Wednesday, August 1, 2007
By Mike Harris

GORDON WINS AT TALLADEGA
Talladega, Alabama, Monday, October 8, 2007
By Jenna Fryer

MARCH CONTINUES TOWARD 5TH NEXTEL CUP TITLE
Concord, North Carolina, Sunday, October 14, 2007
By Jenna Fryer

BEST OF FRIENDS BATTLE FOR ULTIMATE PRIZE
Hampton, Georgia, Monday, October 29, 2007
By Paul Newberry

JOHNSON TAKES COMMAND OF TITLE CHASE
Avondale, Arizona, Monday, November 12, 2007
By Jenna Fryer

JOHNSON AND GORDON STILL FAST FRIENDS
Homestead, Florida, Thursday, November 15, 2007
By Mike Harris

Chapter 5. PERSONAL LIFE

GORDON CONFIRMS DIVORCE FILING
Charlotte, North Carolina, Monday, March 18, 2002
By The Associated Press

COUNTERSUES WIFE FOR DIVORCE
West Palm Beach, Florida, Thursday, April 11, 2002
By The Associated Press

'THE KID' NOW GOING IT ALONE
Charlotte, North Carolina, Saturday, April 20, 2002
By Jenna Fryer

CONFIDENTIALITY AGREEMENT
West Palm Beach, Florida, Thursday, May 9, 2002
By The Associated Press

GORDON SPORTS GOATEE
Concord, North Carolina, Monday, May 17, 2002
By Jenna Fryer

GORDON WORTH $48.8 MILLION
Delray Beach, Florida, Friday, December 20, 2002
By The Associated Press

LAWYERS TRY TO SERVE SUBPOENAS AT DAYTONA
Daytona Beach, Florida, Monday, February 10, 2003
By Jenna Fryer

DIVORCE SETTLEMENT
West Palm Beach, Florida, Sunday, June 15, 2003
By The Associated Press

GORDON MARRIES SECOND WIFE
Charlotte, North Carolina, Wednesday, November 8, 2006
By The Associated Press

FATHERHOOD
Birmingham, Alabama, Wednesday, March 28, 2007
By John Zenor

BABY GIRL
New York, Wednesday, June 20, 2007
By The Associated Press

LIFE'S GOOD
Charlotte, North Carolina, Saturday, June 23, 2007
By Jenna Fryer

SECOND CHILD
Daytona Beach, Florida, Thursday, February 4, 2010
By The Associated Press

FINAL LAP FOR 'FOUR-TIME'
Charlotte, North Carolina, Sunday, June 28, 2015
By The Associated Press

THE AP EMERGENCY RELIEF FUND

When Hurricane Katrina hit the Gulf Coast in 2005, many Associated Press staffers and their families were personally affected. AP employees rallied to help these colleagues by setting up the AP Emergency Relief Fund, which has become a source of crucial assistance for the past 10 years.

Established as an independent 501(c)(3), the Fund helps AP staffers who have suffered damage or losses as a result of conflict or natural disasters. These grants are used to rebuild homes, move to safe houses and repair and replace bomb-damaged belongings.

The AP matches all gifts in full and also donates the net proceeds from AP Essentials, AP's company store, to the Fund.

HOW TO GIVE

In order to be ready to help the moment emergencies strike, the Fund relies on the generous and ongoing support of the extended AP community. All donations are matched in full by The Associated Press and can be made any time at http://www.ap.org/relieffund and are tax deductible.

On behalf of the AP staffers and families who receive aid in times of crisis, the AP Emergency Relief Fund Directors and Officers thank you.

ALSO AVAILABLE FROM AP EDITIONS

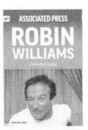

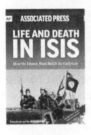